THE YOUNG PERSON'S GUIDE TO AUTISTIC BURNOUT

of related interest

So, I'm Autistic
An Introduction to Autism for Young Adults and Late Teens
Sarah O'Brien
ISBN 978 1 83997 226 3
eISBN 978 1 83997 227 0
Audiobook ISBN 978 1 39981 989 3

The Teen's Guide to PDA
Laura Kerbey
Illustrated by Eliza Fricker
ISBN 978 1 80501 183 5
eISBN 978 1 80501 184 2

Being Autistic (And What That Actually Means)
Niamh Garvey
Illustrated by Rebecca Burgess
ISBN 978 1 80501 171 2
eISBN 978 1 80501 172 9

The Young Person's Guide to Autistic Burnout

Viv Dawes

Illustrated by Josh Dawes

Jessica Kingsley Publishers
London and Philadelphia

First published in Great Britain in 2025 by Jessica Kingsley Publishers
An imprint of John Murray Press

1

Copyright © Viv Dawes 2025

The right of Viv Dawes to be identified as the Author of the Work has been asserted by her in accordance with the Copyright, Designs and Patents Act 1988.

Front cover image source: Josh Dawes.

All rights reserved. No part of this publication may be reproduced, stored in a retrieval system, or transmitted, in any form or by any means without the prior written permission of the publisher, nor be otherwise circulated in any form of binding or cover other than that in which it is published and without a similar condition being imposed on the subsequent purchaser.

The fonts, layout and overall design of this book have been prepared according to dyslexia friendly principles. At JKP we aim to make our books' content accessible to as many readers as possible.

A CIP catalogue record for this title is available from the British Library and the Library of Congress

ISBN 978 1 80501 732 5
eISBN 978 1 80501 733 2

Printed and bound in Great Britain by Bell & Bain Limited

Jessica Kingsley Publishers' policy is to use papers that are natural, renewable and recyclable products and made from wood grown in sustainable forests. The logging and manufacturing processes are expected to conform to the environmental regulations of the country of origin.

Jessica Kingsley Publishers
Carmelite House
50 Victoria Embankment
London EC4Y 0DZ

www.jkp.com

John Murray Press
Part of Hodder & Stoughton Ltd
An Hachette Company

The authorised representative in the EEA is Hachette Ireland,
8 Castlecourt Centre, Dublin 15, D15 XTP3, Ireland (email: info@hbgi.ie)

Contents

Introduction	7
Luna and Jordan: An Introduction	10

PART 1: UNDERSTANDING AUTISM

1.	What Are Neurodiversity and Neurodivergence?	**14**
2.	What Is Autism?	**17**
	Luna and Jordan: What It's Like Being Autistic	27
3.	Understanding Our Autistic Brains	**32**
	Luna and Jordan: How They Feel About Their Interests	35

PART 2: UNDERSTANDING AUTISTIC BURNOUT

4.	What Is Autistic Burnout?	**38**
	Luna and Jordan: What Burnout Feels Like	47
5.	Some of the Main Causes of Autistic Burnout	**50**
	Luna and Jordan: Feeling Like They Can't Be Themselves	56
6.	Masking	**59**
7.	Demands and Expectations	**63**

8. Running Out of Energy — **69**
　　Luna and Jordan: People, Places, and Things
　　That Use Up Spoons — 72

9. School — **74**
　　Luna and Jordan: School and Autistic Burnout — 76

10. The P Word: Puberty and Autistic Burnout — **81**
　　Luna and Jordan: Puberty — 84

11. When Emotions and Feelings Are Big and Confusing — **87**

12. All Our Different Senses — **94**
　　Luna and Jordan: Emotional and Sensory Overload — 99

PART 3: RECOVERY, PREVENTION, AND LOOKING AHEAD

13. Recovery and Prevention — **104**
　　Luna and Jordan: Recovery — 111

14. Stories of Hope — **114**

　　Helpful Books and Websites — 121

　　Glossary — 122

　　References — 128

Introduction

I wonder if you are reading this book because perhaps you have already heard about autistic burnout and you are intrigued to find out more? Or your parent/carer, or someone supporting you, has given it to you to read?

This might be because they think you could be struggling currently with what could be autistic burnout or because it's something they want you to know more about, so you can understand any experiences you have in the future. It is something that many autistic people go through, including myself, my son Josh, and the characters in this book, Luna and Jordan.

So, if you are having a difficult time as an autistic person at the moment (or you suspect that you are autistic) and are experiencing burnout – you are most definitely not alone.

You do not need an official diagnosis to identify as autistic, many autistic people self-identify (also known as self-diagnosis). An official diagnosis, if you get one, is usually given by a psychologist who is part of a specialist team.

There are positives about having an *official* diagnosis, as there are things that you might be less likely to access without one, such as disability benefits; in the UK this would include Disability Living Allowance and Personal Independence Payments (PIP is for when you are post 16).

It can be *easier* to access support in education via something called an EHCP in the UK, or IEP in the US, when there is an official diagnosis; an EHCP is an Education and Health Care Plan and is a support plan for your health/mental health and education needs, that goes with you up until you are 25 years old.

My aim is for this book to help young autistic people like you to understand what autistic burnout is, why it happens and how things can improve. Although life might be really hard for you at the moment, things can and will change and I want to encourage you with some stories of hope, which you will find at the end of the book. If you are reading this book and you're feeling in a good place I hope that the advice will prevent you experiencing burnout in the future, or help you to recognise it early when it happens, so that you can put some things in place.

The book will explain a little about what it means to be autistic too, as I believe that embracing our differences can *really* help us not only to better understand ourselves but to know what our needs are as neurodivergent people. If that's the first time you have come across the word 'neurodivergent', I will explain what it means later.

Although I write about things that affect our physical, emotional, and mental wellbeing as autistic people, I am not a doctor, a mental health practitioner, or a medical professional of any kind. I am, however, autistic (and have attention deficit hyperactivity disorder – ADHD) myself; I didn't find out until I was much older. I have many years' experience of helping and supporting other neurodivergent people. I am also the parent of an autistic teenager who is 18. He has been through burnout and is now in recovery; in fact he did the illustrations for this book and is now embarking on a career in the arts. You can read about his story later in the book.

I hope this book sheds some light upon the stuff that you need to better understand yourself and how burnout can make you feel. We hope that it helps your family and friends too, so that they can provide support in ways that work for you.

The two characters Luna and Jordan were created and illustrated by my son Josh. We hope you can identify with these characters, as they tell you about their life, their experiences of autistic burnout, and how they started to feel better.

Luna and Jordan:
An Introduction

Jordan and Luna are good friends. They regularly chat with each other on Instagram and WhatsApp and sometimes game together, although Jordan is more into gaming than Luna. Because they are both autistic they feel comfortable with each other and feel free talking about being neurodivergent.

Luna **Jordan**

Luna (they/them) is 16 years old and lives with their adopted mum and their pet dog 'Harry'. They have recently been diagnosed as autistic and have strongly believed they are autistic since they were 14.

They have an EHCP (Education and Health Care Plan) and they are going to an alternative school where they get to spend time with farm animals, are able to do horse riding, and enjoy feeding the chickens.

Luna has a new friend that they met when they were at school who is also autistic and they both enjoy drawing, painting, sharing funny memes, and watching things like *Stranger Things* and Marvel films.

Jordan (he/him) is 15 years old and lives at home with his mum, dad, and his little brother Malachi. He has been diagnosed as autistic since he was 7 and ADHD since he was 10. His mum is also autistic and Jordan thinks his dad and brother are also definitely autistic. He has been out of mainstream school for 18 months due to going through autistic burnout.

Jordan enjoys gaming, listening to music, and reading fantasy novels. He likes to meet up online with a small group of friends to play games; they are also mostly all autistic and ADHD young people. Because he finds social situations stressful and exhausting he spends a lot of time at home and often alone in his bedroom. This is because he often gets really tired and overwhelmed.

PART I
UNDERSTANDING AUTISM

CHAPTER 1

What Are Neurodiversity and Neurodivergence?

There is this wonderful thing called 'The Neurodiversity Paradigm'. A paradigm is a set of concepts, ideas, and theories about something. Neurodiversity is the understanding that all humans have different types of brains. If you think of neurodiversity as a huge umbrella that every brain sits under, then also under that umbrella are brains that are different. These brains are known as neurodivergent – they are neurologically divergent from 'typical' brains.

Autistic people (and other neurodivergent people) have been finding better ways to describe themselves and about having different brains. 'The terms *neurodivergent* and *neurodivergence* were coined in the year 2000 by Kassiane Asasumasu, a multiply neurodivergent neurodiversity activist' (Stimpunks Foundation n.d.).

Neurodivergent people are those whose brains differ or diverge from neurotypical brains – thought by many to be the predominant type of brain. Many neurodivergent people are what's known as *multiply* neurodivergent, for example people who are autistic and dyslexic, dyspraxic, or, as we have already mentioned, ADHD.

WHAT ARE NEURODIVERSITY AND NEURODIVERGENCE?

There are many brains that are known as neurodivergent *including*:

- autistic
- ADHD (attention deficit hyperactivity disorder)
- PDA (pathological demand avoidance)
- OCD (obsessive compulsive disorder)
- dyslexic
- dyspraxic
- Tourette's syndrome.

As you can see, a lot of the ways that neurodivergent brains are described use words such as *disorder* and *syndrome*. This is because these neurotypes (brain types) were first discovered by medical professionals such as psychiatrists and psychologists many years ago and were described using medical terms. Many neurodivergent people are trying to find better ways to describe the different kinds of brains, for example PDA is described by many as a 'persistent drive for autonomy'.

An autistic psychologist, educator, and author called Dr Nick Walker writes a lot about this topic and you can find out loads about being neurodivergent and the best language to use on her website https://neuroqueer.com/neurodiversity-terms-and-definitions.

Dr Nick Walker (n.d.) explains:

> Neurodiversity is the diversity of human minds.... a natural and valuable form of human diversity.
>
> Neurodivergent, sometimes abbreviated as ND, means

15

having a mind that functions in ways which diverge significantly from the dominant societal standards of 'normal'.

The correct way therefore to describe an autistic person is that they are neurodivergent and not neurodiverse, as many mistakenly describe us.

Neuro*diverse* describes *all* the different kinds of human brains. Dr Walker, however, also explains that 'There are countless possible ways to be neurodivergent, and being autistic is only one of those ways.'

CHAPTER 2
What Is Autism?

> The world needs to understand that being Autistic is different to being typical, but not different to being human. As a human being, we have talents, strengths and interests that can be the foundation for a positive self-worth.
>
> **DR WENN LAWSON (ACERBECKY 2015)**

I think it's important for everyone to understand autism and what being autistic means. This is because there are a lot of myths and stereotypes about autism out there that can lead to autistic people being stigmatised. These myths mean people often think things about autistic people that are untrue and misleading, such as believing that autistic people can't socialise or that they don't have

emotions, empathy, or an imagination. People can even believe that all autistic people are brilliant at maths, and I don't know about you but I am rubbish at maths, so that definitely isn't true!

So I want to start by explaining what autism is to help you appreciate your differently wired brain.

When we first discover or are told by a professional that we are autistic it might feel a bit scary; we might feel something is wrong with us. I want to reassure you that there is absolutely nothing wrong with you or your brain, you are not broken, it is just a *different* type of brain.

Some amazing things about being autistic

An eye for detail
Autistic people have what's known as 'monotropic' brains and tend to focus very intensely on a smaller number of things at a time. This can mean we often see things that other people (who aren't autistic) don't see.

Rather than being 'top-down' thinkers, autistic people are what's known as 'bottom-up' thinkers, which means autistic people will tend to focus on detail before we can focus on the bigger picture. This is also how we learn. Our unique way of seeing the world means we can engage with life in a refreshingly different way.

Problem solving
Because of our ability to focus on detail, it can mean autistic

people are great at problem solving. We see patterns in many things and this helps us form what are often very creative ideas and solutions.

Passionate
Autistic people's brains and nervous systems are what's known as interest-based and they can become intensely, deeply focused on a few interests. This is also linked to what's known as being 'monotropic', which I will explain in more detail later in the book.

Often concerned about justice
It is very common for autistic people to feel strongly about issues relating to justice, whether that's social justice or animal rights, etc. A great example of an autistic person like this is Greta Thunberg. Feeling passionately about something and being prepared to stand up for what's right can change the world!

Kind and caring
A lot of autistic people are involved in caring for others, become therapists, counsellors, nurses, doctors, paramedics, etc. For many autistic people honesty and integrity is also really important. All of this can make us very reliable and highly thought of as friends and work colleagues.

In-depth knowledge
Because of the tendency to focus intensely on a few interests, autistic people often learn and retain a lot of in-depth knowledge and understanding about these things. We can truly become experts and advanced thinkers in our chosen fields.

Tenacious

Autistic people can be extremely tenacious and very determined. Have you heard the term 'like a dog with a bone'? Well, that's what a lot of autistic people can be like about things that are important to them. This can be an important trait that helps us to get to the bottom of problems, even when there are barriers in the way.

Creative and innovative

It is really common for autistic people to be very creative and there are some amazing autistic authors, artists, actors, dancers, and musicians, for example.

A great example of a very gifted autistic person who is creative is the amazing British artist Stephen Wiltshire. You can check out his story and his artwork here: www.stephenwiltshire.co.uk. There are some extremely innovative autistic people who have created and developed amazing new ideas, designs, inventions, and concepts, such as Temple Grandin, who is an autistic scientist.

How to describe autism

It is important to understand that autism is not a medical or a mental health condition or problem, as people can wrongly assume. Autism is also not a learning disability, although an autistic person can have a learning disability such as dyslexia as well.

Some people refer to autism as a disorder: autistic spectrum disorder (ASD) or a condition (ASC). But the words disorder and condition are not helpful or affirming ways

WHAT IS AUTISM?

to understand and explain autism; these descriptions can leave you feeling that something is wrong with you – which there isn't.

Many professionals that you will come into contact with, such as teachers, doctors, psychologists, social workers etc., tend to refer to autism as ASD, which is *medical model* language. They also might use what's known as 'person first' language, which describes people as *having autism*, rather than 'identity first language' which describes someone as *autistic*.

Language is important and most autistic people (80% plus in surveys) actually prefer 'identity first' language, which sounds like 'I am autistic'. This is because autism is not something a person 'has' but is in fact an identity, although you can choose what terminology you feel most comfortable with.

When people have an assessment for autism, the report that is written by a psychologist will use terms and words such as impairments, deficits, abnormal, dysfunctional, obsessions, and difficulties. I and many other autistic people think these words are unhelpful and horrible ways to describe autistic minds! They can make autistic people feel like we are abnormal in some way but there is no such thing as an abnormal brain.

Being autistic means a person has a *different* kind of brain, also known as a 'neurotype', and not a *broken* type of brain. Being autistic does not mean you need to be fixed or changed. Autistic people experience, process, and express everything differently, whether that is how they communicate, how they experience their senses, the interests they have, or even how they socialise.

Autism is naturally occurring and commonly runs in families too. I like to describe being autistic as being a person who has a different type of lens – like a lens in a camera. It means I see and experience myself, others, and the world differently to people who are not autistic.

Sometimes people describe autistic people as being high or low functioning, or even as being mildly or severely autistic. These terms can be harmful. Just because an autistic person is described as 'high functioning' and seems to cope day-to-day (according to society's standards) does not mean that they don't have significant challenges. Sometimes that 'coping' can come at great cost. Equally, describing an autistic person as 'low functioning' is likely to lower expectations around what they can achieve. In actual fact they are likely to be as capable as the next person given the right environment and support.

The autistic spectrum is not like this:

High Functioning ⟷ Low Functioning

The autistic spectrum is not something that is linear, with one end being mild or slightly autistic and the other end being very or severely autistic. It is not something that we are 'on'. Rather, I like to think of the autistic spectrum as a rainbow that goes right through every part of each autistic person, describing all our differences, needs, and strengths.

An autistic person's needs are not fixed, they can change – both over time and throughout a single day. Your needs may be different in the various environments/places you find yourself in. Your support needs at home, for example, can be very different to those in school or college, etc.

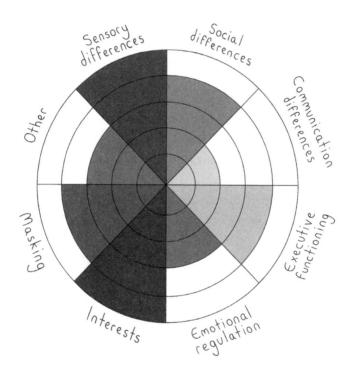

Autistic people have many differences

Differences in our sensory system
Autistic people can have all kinds of sensory differences, such as their experiences of sound, taste, smell, sight, touch, and

also the experience of external and internal body signals such as balance, hunger, thirst, pain, and emotions (this is called interoception, which I will explain later in the book).

Autistic people can be more or less sensitive to different senses, known as being hyper (more) or hypo (less) sensitive. The degree of sensory sensitivity can vary across senses – so you might be hypersensitive to some things and hyposensitive to others.

Differences in communication and socialising

Autistic people can often feel very misunderstood by others who are not autistic. This is often because we communicate differently. For example, it's not uncommon for autistic people to be very literal, to find eye contact hard, and to avoid small talk about mundane everyday things (because, let's face it, small talk is boring and irrelevant). Autistic people often prefer to connect through their interests and things they feel passionate about and may 'info-dump' and talk enthusiastically about things they are hyperfocused on.

Sometimes, when an autistic person is trying to explain something to a neurotypical person (a person with a more common type of brain), it can feel a bit like two computers with different operating systems trying to communicate. This is due to something Dr Damian Milton (an autistic academic) calls 'the problem of double empathy'. This means that when people with different life experiences try to understand each other they can struggle to have empathy for the other person. Neither side is wrong, and neither should assume that the other should be the one to change – great communication is around accommodations and understanding on *both* sides.

Autistic people have different levels of capacity for social situations. It means that social situations can be quite taxing and sometimes just talking can be exhausting for autistic people. Some autistic people cannot talk in certain situations, this is known as *situational mutism*. Also, some autistic people do not use speech to communicate at all, but this does not mean they do not have 'a voice' – remember communication is not just verbal.

Autistic people may find certain social situations more exhausting to be in than others, particularly when those situations are busy, noisy, and overwhelming and where there are perhaps too many things to focus on. It is also not unusual for autistic people to feel that they don't belong or fit in with others who are not autistic or otherwise neurodivergent.

Differences in interests

Autistic people often have intense interests and passions that they become really absorbed in; sometimes these interests last for days or weeks, but for many they last for a long time, even a lifetime. This is because autistic people have what's called 'monotropic' brains – a brain that focuses more intensely on a smaller number of things. These interests might be very different to your peers' interests but that's absolutely ok. Different is never wrong.

Differences in executive functioning

There is a part of the human brain called the prefrontal cortex. This is wired differently in people who are autistic and also in people who are ADHD. It's a part of the brain that controls some of the most important functions related to 'thinking' (also known as cognition). These are things such as decision making, working memory, motivation, planning and organising things, starting and finishing things, emotional regulation, self-control, and focus.

Differences in this part of the brain mean autistic people often need more time to process information, for example, and have unique ways of focusing. This can use up lots of energy. They may find it hard to start things and can sometimes feel stuck and not know how to stop. They may become emotionally overwhelmed more easily and not always know how to regulate. Sometimes they will need to regulate with another person (known as co-regulation).

Many autistic people are also ADHD (often known as AuDHD). For these people, their differences can also mean they might find organising themselves, remembering things and making plans much harder – although some AuDHD people (like me!) are extremely organised with some tasks and struggle with motivation around others.

Focusing and regulating (regulation means to change the intensity of how you feel and experience something) might feel much more challenging for someone who is AuDHD and they may need a lot more movement in order to help them regulate. This is because movement is important for the release of dopamine – which is a chemical in the brain that helps with mood, motivation, memory, sleep, focus, and lots of other functions.

Luna and Jordan:
What It's Like Being Autistic

Luna

> I thought I was autistic for a long time before I got my official diagnosis recently. At first, although I knew I might be autistic I didn't like it much, as I thought it meant that there was something wrong with me. This is apparently called 'internalised ableism'. I didn't want anyone at school knowing because I was scared what other people might think, including the teachers!
>
> After my diagnosis it has been a relief, as I finally had an answer to the reason as to why I am different. I read a few books by autistic people that helped me start to understand what being autistic means. I am now starting to understand what I need more and more and also what I don't need. I watch YouTube videos by neurodivergent creators and this has helped me to accept myself.
>
> School didn't think I was autistic as according to them

'I was fine in school.' I can't believe they thought this. I was not fine. I might have seemed fine on the surface but underneath I was really struggling especially in secondary school. On the outside I smiled, gave eye contact, didn't break any rules, and did all my schoolwork and homework. But on the inside I was overwhelmed and anxious because I am aways taking everything in wherever I am.

I often feel like I don't know what other people expect of me, like all the other people at school seemed to know what was expected and I had to try to work it all out. Now I understand that that's because I experience everything differently, but school and lots of other places are not designed for minds that are different like mine.

I am often very quiet and sometimes I don't speak at all; people used to say this was just because I was shy, but actually I sometimes don't speak because I am really anxious and exhausted. I am not being rude or 'just being a teenager' – I really cannot communicate at these times. My mum used to try to make me talk when I felt like this and this made things worse. Now she knows it's best to let me be; she checks I am safe but she knows I need time alone and sometimes it can last for days (or even longer when I am in burnout).

I love that I am autistic! I am different and that's not a horrible thing. That doesn't mean that I don't get anxious or get tired, because I do, but now I know why. I think it's important that schools and other places understand autistic people like me, so that we feel accepted for who we are rather than trying to make us fit in and be neurotypical.

I wish others didn't believe stupid things about autism such as that we don't have empathy for others, I really care about other people and think about them all the time. I also really love animals and they help me, especially my pet dog Harry who I adore more than anything. Being around animals makes me feel that nothing bad is going to happen and that I can just be me.**"**

Jordan

"I was first told I was autistic when I was little; I was 7 I think and at junior school. Apparently, the teachers noticed things about me that meant I wasn't like the other children in the class. My mum told me it was because I played on my own and hardly spoke or looked at anyone. I am still like that really – I do not like looking at people and I don't like it when people make me look at them. I am also a really quiet person. I don't talk much, even at home. I mostly like to be in my room, reading or gaming.

I know people have different ideas about autism and a lot of those people are not even autistic! I don't like this, as how can you really understand something and what it's like unless you experience it? My mum and dad have different views about autism and that can get a bit confusing; my dad is probably neurodivergent but he doesn't think so and gets a bit annoyed if anyone says anything to him about 'probably being autistic'.

My mum is diagnosed as autistic. In fact, apparently as soon as I got my diagnosis she went to her doctor and said she wanted to find out about herself also. My dad wasn't very impressed but, anyway, she got a diagnosis. My brother is younger than me and I think he is definitely autistic as he is starting to struggle in school like I did.

I don't like the way people think autistic people like me are weird and compare us to robots, saying things like we can't make friends. I do have friends, not loads, but they are mostly other autistic people. They are the friends I feel comfortable with because they are like me, they accept me, and they don't say horrible things to me either.

A lot of the other people in school used to ignore me and treated me like I had some sort of disease. I would often sit on my own at lunchtime and all the teachers would say is that I needed to try to be more sociable and join in. This made me feel stupid and even weirder – of course I can try to be 'sociable' but I am not interested in football or girlfriends and being in a big group of other teenagers all staring at me waiting for me to speak feels horrible! All that would happen is that I would panic, get overwhelmed, and they would end up laughing at me and walk off leaving me on my own again.

Being autistic can sometimes be really hard in a world

where you don't feel you fit, because you can get bullied and left out of things. The teachers in school really didn't understand what I found hard and didn't know what would have helped me, they just kept telling me to focus and look at them, to engage better in class and stop fidgeting.

My mum being diagnosed as autistic has helped me to accept myself more, plus she has read lots of books and been to lots of courses. She tells me all the things that she learns about autism and ADHD also. I am different to her as I am much quieter but I can see that she feels confident being herself and that makes me feel happy. ”

CHAPTER 3

Understanding Our Autistic Brains

Autistic people have monotropic brains. You might have never heard the words monotropic or monotropism before, so let me explain what it means: if you break the word down, the first part 'mono' means one. So there is your clue. Monotropic brains process things more intensely and they focus on *one* or a few things at a time. People who are not neurodivergent, however, are more likely to have brains that can focus on lots of things all at the same time and these are called polytropic brains.

Autistic people often have one or a few interests and passions that they are really strongly focused on. When I was a child I would spend literally hours birdwatching and copying pictures from the books I read about birds from all around the world. I could spend all day just doing this and my interest carried on for years; I still know the names of birds just by hearing their calls. I still learn this way – one thing at a time, really intensely. Maybe you have one or a few interests that you like to spend lots of time focused on, thinking about, and talking about?

Many people, not just autistic people, can get really focused on something and this is known as being hyperfocused. They can end up in what's called an 'attention tunnel' and they enter what some refer to as a 'flow state'. For autistic people and other neurodivergent people this can be so much more intense! I like to call my attention tunnels 'wormholes'.

In my wormholes I can feel safe, reassured, and happy too. The downside, I suppose, is that I can get so lost in my wormhole that everything outside of that attention tunnel becomes like someone pressed the mute button on the TV remote. I lose track of time; I don't connect to the signals from my body telling me that I am hungry or thirsty and even that I need to use the toilet sometimes. Maybe you can relate to that?

Some people describe an autistic person's nervous system as 'interest based'. So those interests that you are really focused on are not obsessions but are due to the way you are wired. As long as your interests help you feel good about yourself and about others, make you happy and feel content, then that's really great. These interests can help restore lost energy too and a shared special interest with another autistic person can feel amazing!

Having a monotropic brain isn't just to do with special interests though, it actually means that everything can be very intense – our thoughts, emotions, senses, and everything about us. Sometimes we might also experience and focus intensely on what are known as 'intrusive thoughts'. Intrusive thoughts are unwanted negative thoughts, and sometimes also feelings, that seem to come out of nowhere. These can be a sign of anxiety, but in some people they can also be a sign of something called OCD (obsessive compulsive disorder). If you have thoughts of needing to do a certain thing over and over (some call this a ritual) and you believe something awful will happen if you don't do it, then it would be a good idea to talk to an adult about this, maybe discuss it with your parents; it's not uncommon for autistic people to have OCD.

There is therapy available for OCD, but it's really important to make sure that this therapy is suitable for an autistic person (this is therapy that is 'neuro affirming') and that you have any therapy at the right time as talking can be exhausting for autistic people, especially in burnout.

Getting stuck in looping intrusive thoughts as an autistic person can be really common and can leave you feeling overwhelmed and dysregulated. Being emotionally dysregulated means having difficulty in adjusting your emotions. I like to think of regulating emotions as like when you use a dimmer switch, which doesn't turn the light off but can dim the light. So, this means that being regulated doesn't mean trying to be completely calm but that the emotions you experience are *dimmed* and not so intense. We will look at what can help you regulate your emotions later in the book.

All that intensity when you have a monotropic brain can be exhausting – even when you are focused on things you love! This is why autistic people are more prone to experiencing burnout. Sometimes we get stuck in our wormholes and find it hard to leave and that is why it is important to learn to pace ourselves. Sometimes we need others to gently remind us to take breaks, to remember to eat and drink and maybe go out for a walk if we can.

Luna and Jordan:
How They Feel About Their Interests

Luna

"My interests are mainly drawing Marvel characters and watching *Stranger Things*. I regularly re-watch the whole series with my best friend and then we spend hours talking about it and deconstructing the characters.

I can also get really focused on drawing characters from my favourite Marvel films. Sometimes it's like I just get stuck and I can't move. Other times I really want to draw but I just can't. I hate it when this happens as it makes me feel even more tired. Often a bit later in the day suddenly out of nowhere I find myself there again, in my cocoon with

> my paper and pencils. There are days, however, when I just sleep loads probably because I need the rest. I have days when I am super hyperfocused and don't do anything else; this can be really helpful for me as I don't worry about anything else, but I have to be aware that even this can also exhaust me.

Jordan

> I love gaming, listening to music and reading fantasy novels. I wear my noise cancelling headphones to listen to my favourite playlists and this can also help me sleep. I spend hours and hours playing *Zelda* and other games that I play online with my friends. This is definitely when I feel happiest and most chilled, but I find it hard when I am interrupted.
>
> I really hate it when I am super hyperfocused on a game and then suddenly my mum or dad shouts up at me that I need to come and eat dinner or feed the cat or something. I can feel really angry! Sometimes I have ended up in a meltdown because I have found it so hard to change from playing the game to doing something else too quickly. This happened a lot in school, when I was focused on something in one lesson and then suddenly expected to just go to another lesson and be focused again. It made me feel really tired all the time.

PART II
UNDERSTANDING AUTISTIC BURNOUT

CHAPTER 4

What Is Autistic Burnout?

A utistic burnout is something that can happen to any autistic person. There are many physical, emotional, and mental characteristics of autistic burnout. It can feel like something has sucked all the energy out of you – a bit like when your phone battery runs out of juice, the phone can't function any longer. Like the phone battery that can no longer run the phone, lots of things change during burnout and you might find you are unable to do the things you used to do.

According to researcher Dora Raymaker:

> Autistic burnout is a state of physical and mental fatigue, heightened stress, and diminished capacity to manage life skills, sensory input, and/or social interactions, which comes from years of being severely overtaxed by the strain of trying to live up to demands that are out of sync with our needs. (Raymaker *et al.* 2020)

You might experience the following:

- You are so physically and mentally exhausted that it

WHAT IS AUTISTIC BURNOUT?

Masking differences Sensory overload Emotionally overwhelmed

Traumatised Demands

Hyperarousal

Meltdowns increase Shutdowns increase
Changes in eating
Self-care affected

Feeling unsafe

Can't focus

Vomiting Shaking Headaches
Anxiety Stomach aches

No energy

Hypoarousal No more energy
for masking
Can't attend
school

Mental health worsens

Self-harm
Intrusive thoughts

Suicidal
thoughts

Exhausted

No
resources
left

Crash

might even be difficult or even impossible to get out of bed some or most days.

- It is much harder to remember certain things, process your thoughts, make decisions and plans.

- There might be lots of things you cannot do anymore, things that you used to do more easily or loved doing.

- You are finding it really challenging to focus.

- You may find it's very hard to regulate your emotions.

- You may feel extremely anxious and you may also feel very low in mood.

- Your sensory overload has increased, and you might also seek out more sensory experiences too (known as sensory seeking).

- You can find communicating with other people much harder, even with your family and friends and talking may stop altogether. You might feel really *shut down*, numb, and disconnected.

- Being around people feels really difficult, especially as talking, engaging, and answering questions feels really overwhelming, even impossible.

- Many everyday demands including things like having a shower, getting dressed, or brushing your teeth may feel much harder to do.

- You might struggle with eating or may eat more and find yourself bingeing.

- Sleeping may change loads. You might sleep more or struggle with sleeping at all. Many autistic people find that during burnout they become nocturnal (sleeping for most of the day and being awake at night).

- Some people struggle with a lot of, or a lot more, intrusive thoughts during burnout.

If you are hurting yourself and/or having worrying intrusive thoughts about yourself and your life there are helplines you can contact on the websites mentioned at the end of the book. If you can talk to a parent or carer then it's really important that they know. If you cannot speak about this then maybe message them instead. Remember you are not a bad person, you are experiencing big and overwhelming emotions, and you don't have to carry all this on your own.

All of the experiences during burnout might mean you might want to just be alone in your bedroom with your curtains shut and want everyone to just leave you alone. Doing the simplest things can be so demanding and exhausting. Some people call doing this during burnout 'hibernating'.

An autistic advocate called Judy Endow describes autistic burnout as the result of 'years of being severely overtaxed by the strain of trying to live up to demands that are out of sync with your needs'.

In other words, when environments such as schools and

colleges don't understand autistic young people's specific and unique needs, it means you are forced like square pegs into round holes. The result of being forced to be in environments that are not suitable for autistic people causes trauma.

When experiencing burnout, autistic people commonly find they no longer have the energy to mask their differences anymore. This can lead to increases in meltdowns and shutdowns. It's also important to say here that meltdowns are not tantrums, as some people wrongly believe. They are in fact a sign that the autistic person is really anxious and overwhelmed; they are an involuntary fight/flight response of the nervous system. Meltdowns are not something that you can always control and are exhausting.

Shutdowns are also misunderstood but like meltdowns are a sign of extreme anxiety. They are an involuntary freeze response of the nervous system. The autistic person usually stops being able to talk or communicate, withdraws socially, and may not be able to move.

A lot of people may think that autistic burnout is depression, and there are a lot of similarities but they are not the same thing. That's not to say that an autistic person cannot feel depressed when they are going through burnout, as they can.

However, treating autistic burnout as if it is depression can have a very negative impact upon the person and could prolong burnout or make it worse. To help a person experiencing depression a doctor or CAMHS (Child and Adolescent Mental Health Services in the UK), for example, might prescribe medication, recommend certain therapies like cognitive behavioural therapy (CBT), suggest they see more people, go out and do more. What helps with autistic burnout, however, is very different.

Survival mode and shutting down

When you are experiencing autistic burnout it is because your nervous system has been in survival mode for such a long time. In this mode your brain is getting the message that you are in danger all the time.

Survival mode is our brain's natural way of dealing with things like fear, stress, and trauma and is also known as the fight, flight, freeze, fawn, flop response.

Fight – experiencing meltdowns, feeling very overwhelmed and extremely angry. It might lead to shouting or screaming. Sometimes we might feel all this internally but don't express it.

Flight – running away, escaping the situation we are overwhelmed by, sometimes during a meltdown.

Freeze – shutting down, feeling exhausted, becoming quiet, still, numb.

Fawn – a way to stay safe and avoid conflict with others by people pleasing and putting other people's needs first.

Flop – when people are extremely anxious they can sometimes faint.

These *involuntary* responses are triggered by something in the most primitive part of our brain, called the amygdala, which is in the limbic system (the part of the brain that controls things like how we deal with fear and many other functions).

The amygdala is a kind of alarm system that tells the brain and nervous system that you are in danger. It responds to real or imagined danger in the same way. This alarm system triggers the release of all sorts of chemicals into the bloodstream, like the stress chemical cortisol and adrenaline (teenagers generally have higher levels of cortisol). Essentially your brain does this because it is always trying to keep us safe.

Shutdowns happen when you are experiencing a *freeze* response and can include having no energy, withdrawing from others, not being able to focus, feeling detached, not being able to talk or communicate, and maybe even finding it hard to physically move.

In a shutdown an autistic person may also feel very low, experience intrusive thoughts and even physical symptoms such as headaches, joint pain, or stomach problems. Shutdowns can feel scary and it's important when experiencing this that you are supported with compassion and without judgement. It is not something that you can help happening and is not something you can stop. Shutdowns do, however, come to an end and do not last forever.

Hibernation and going nocturnal

To reset a computer you have to restart it by turning it off and then back on again, and hibernating for many is the nervous system's way of repairing and resetting during autistic burnout. It may look like you burrowing away in your bedroom with the curtains closed, withdrawing from others, and staying in bed longer. This response is really common and, if this is what you are experiencing, I want you to know that you are not alone. It does change in time as you reset, repair, and heal.

Sleep is commonly difficult for autistic and other neurodivergent people; they can sometimes have sleep disorders. Sleep issues may also be because of having differences in what's known as the 'circadian rhythm'. The circadian rhythm is 'a natural process in animals and plants that controls when things such as sleeping, eating or growing happen during a 24 hour period' (Cambridge Dictionary, n.d. b).

Melatonin is a chemical that is naturally present in our body and that helps with regulating sleep and waking. Sunshine helps with boosting our natural melatonin levels and some people even use lamps known as 'daylight lamps' (not everyone likes these, however). Some autistic people are prescribed small quantities of melatonin to help with sleep. If you are prescribed this, or you are thinking about it, then it's always important to consult a doctor as melatonin tablets or gummies are still sleep medication.

Sleep can become especially challenging during autistic burnout and many people become nocturnal, sleeping during the day and being awake at night. There are many reasons for this, as being awake at night can mean:

- you experience less sensory overload as it is usually quieter at night
- you have more autonomy

- you don't have to talk or communicate
- there are fewer or no demands and expectations
- you might feel safer within yourself.

Neurotypical strategies for helping with sleep challenges (often called sleep hygiene) might not always work when you are autistic and definitely won't help when you are experiencing burnout. So any advice should come from someone who understands the autistic experience.

Sometimes sleep doesn't happen because an autistic person hasn't had enough time during the day to spend on their interest and passions. Some people call this 'revenge bedtime procrastination'. This is why it is really important to have time resting with your special interests during the daytime, as this can help to reduce cortisol levels.

Often the more you focus on not being able to sleep the worse it can get; sometimes trying to make yourself sleep at certain times can just be too hard, especially when you are in recovery.

Sometimes we need to be flexible and go with what our body is telling us, especially in burnout. As an autistic person going to bed *to go to sleep* can become a demand, especially if you are a PDAer. So bed needs to be a place you associate with rest and not just the place you struggle to sleep. Remember, if sleep is a struggle for you, sleep is more likely when you and your nervous system feel safer and more regulated.

Luna and Jordan:
What Burnout Feels Like

Luna

"Burnout is horrible. I felt so stuck, frozen and didn't feel able to do anything; literally everything felt like an effort. When I was first in burnout I couldn't get out of my bed, let alone leave my room, some days, because I was so tired. My bedroom became my sanctuary and the place I retreated to when everything felt too much.

I often felt so guilty because school were complaining to my mum about my attendance. I was not able to think, let alone read and focus on conversations, even talking was impossible.

I had lots of intrusive thoughts going round and round my head. These thoughts sometimes made me very scared and sad. It was hard to tell anyone about the thoughts because they made

> me feel bad about myself. Eventually, when I could, I did talk to my mum about them and that was really helpful. She didn't tell me the thoughts were silly, but she listened. This helped me see that sometimes when we are very stressed and shutdown we can experience unhelpful racing thoughts. Talking about them seemed to take the power out of them.
>
> On the days when I had the energy I would just watch my favourite things, curled up with my favourite blanket on the sofa or in my room. As I started to feel I had more energy I would spend most of my time drawing. This really helped me as I love drawing – it makes me feel good about myself.
>
> As soon as I started thinking about school though it felt like I fell back down a deep dark hole. The thought of being back there terrified me so much, that I even had nightmares. 🙶

Jordan

> 🙷 When I first went into burnout I thought it was depression. I felt so cold, demotivated, confused, and I didn't feel able to do any of the things I used to enjoy doing. All I wanted to do was stay in my bedroom and couldn't even change out of my pyjamas for months.
>
> This is all a bit embarrassing to talk about, as I felt ashamed of myself. But I couldn't help being like this. I wasn't being difficult or lazy, which is what my grandparents did think at first. They kept telling my

mum that I just needed to go back to school but there was no way I could do that.

Eating was even hard for me and became a massive demand. My mum and dad got really worried about me and they didn't know where to turn for support at first, as the doctors had never heard of autistic burnout. Mum did buy some vitamins to give me, as she was concerned that I might have deficiencies and the doctors thought this was a good idea.

I felt so detached and didn't have the energy to speak to my friends either, which meant I was quite lonely sometimes. As time passed and my parents let me rest loads (which they were told by an autistic advocate was the best thing for me), I did start gaming with my friends again. This made me feel really good as I had really missed them.

The one thing I did feel able to do all through burnout was listen to music. I don't know what I would have done without it? Music has been there for me all throughout the really hard days and the good days too. 🙰

CHAPTER 5

Some of the Main Causes of Autistic Burnout

Now let's look at some of the main causes of autistic burnout. There are many, but I will just focus on some of the main triggers.

Too many demands

Spending lots of time in pressurised environments (school, college, university, and some workplaces, for example) that are very demanding and overwhelming, with lots of social pressure, too much information, and too many expectations. Also, for many, where there is perhaps a lot of unstructured time, uncertainty, and things happening that are unexpected.

An autistic person can experience lower levels of burnout on a regular basis, even daily, which some call social hangovers. They happen because of being regularly exhausted by too much socialising.

Environments

Spending lots of time in environments that don't understand

and don't acknowledge or accommodate your social, communication, sensory, and executive function differences. This can use up lots of your energy, because you might not, for example, be given enough time to process things, remember things, switch focus, regulate, etc.

In these environments you might experience a lot of sensory overload, because your sensory needs are not understood or met. This can be because the environments are too busy, crowded, noisy, cramped, and unpredictable. In school, for example, it can mean too many people talking all at once, people bumping into you lots, making sudden noises, or wearing strong smelling perfumes or deodorant.

Masking

Masking your differences as an autistic person, because you don't feel included, don't feel a sense of belonging, and don't feel *safe* to be your authentic self or show any discomfort. You might not always be aware that you are masking, as it is mostly subconscious. When I say safe, I don't mean just things like staying safe from bullying, but it's important to understand that your nervous system can respond *very* strongly to situations where you cannot be yourself and actually leads to feeling a sense of threat.

Many autistic people might also mask by suppressing physical, mental, and sensory distress. They may feel people do not believe them if they say they are experiencing pain or discomfort, as maybe in the past people have dismissed them. It's not uncommon for autistic people to have what's known as co-occurring physical conditions such as EDS (Ehlers-Danos syndrome), PoTS (postural orthostatic tachycardia), or hypermobility. All these conditions can include pain and can even cause fatigue too. There are some websites at the end of the book that give more information.

Changes

Changes, also known as transitions. These might be big changes such as going through puberty, going from primary school to secondary school, bereavement, or even lots of small changes throughout a day, which can be really stressful and demanding. Switching focus and suddenly leaving things you are focused on can be hard for an autistic person.

Also, it might be really hard to get into what we described before as 'attention tunnels' or 'flow states' with your interests, because there are so many other demands and things you are expected to focus on and this can also be exhausting. Flow states are a really intense state of hyperfocus and being completely absorbed in what you are doing.

Stigma

There is sadly a lot of stigma around what autism is and what it means to be autistic. 'When someone or something is stigmatised, it means they are treated unfairly by disapproving of them' (Cambridge Dictionary n.d. c).

The negative views about autism and being autistic are due to many of the unfair stereotypical ideas and myths there are about autistic people that are just not true. Some of these ideas about autism come from official sources like something called the DSM(V) – *The Diagnostic and Statistical Manual of Mental Disorders.*

This paints a negative and unhelpful picture of autistic people known as the 'medical model' that has led to many of the harmful myths and stereotypes that exist. Rather than describe our differences, the DSM(V) describes autistic people as having *deficits, impairments, abnormalities and restrictions* in how we socialise, develop and maintain relationships, how we communicate and even describes special interests as fixations that are 'abnormal in intensity'.

The medical model perpetuates the myths there are surrounding autism that are also ableist – when something is ableist it means it is discriminatory against anyone with a disability and in favour of those who are not disabled.

This all means it's often harder for autistic people to just be themselves, be authentic, be *out and proud*, and this is because they can often experience feeling misunderstood, being ridiculed and bullied, excluded and rejected.

Perfectionism

Perfectionism and internalised ableism is something a lot of autistic people can struggle with. We might hide things because we feel we have to be perfect or do things perfectly. We might struggle accepting our differences and think we are stupid or weak because we can't do certain things that we see other people doing. This can lead us to push ourselves beyond our capacity and can be exhausting.

The double empathy problem

'The double empathy problem' is something that Damian Milton (an autistic academic) talks about. Basically, it is the idea that people with different experiences of life (which may be because they have different types of brains) can struggle to understand and empathise with each other.

> Simply put, the theory of the double empathy problem suggests that when people with very different experiences of the world interact with one another, they will struggle to empathise with each other. (Milton 2018)

It is very common for autistic people to feel misunderstood and isolated. Many autistic people struggle with their mental health because it's harder to feel seen, heard, and experience connection with others. This is why finding your neurokin as an autistic person is so important.

Rejection

Rejection sensitivity dysphoria (RSD) can be experienced by autistic and other neurodivergent people and often goes hand in hand with perfectionism. This is severe emotional distress caused by real or imagined rejection by others and can be because of criticism, people not replying to messages, being misunderstood by others, feelings of failure, and many other triggers.

The heartache you can feel can be deeply and unbearably painful. When you experience those feelings of rejection it can feel like you have suddenly fallen into a very dark pit and cannot get out. If you experience RSD a lot, this can definitely be exhausting and could contribute to burnout. There is an article and some tips for what can help with RSD at Autism Understood (https://autismunderstood.co.uk).

Luna and Jordan:
Feeling Like They Can't Be Themselves

Luna

❝When I am anywhere that is not my home, anywhere I do not feel safe to really be myself and openly autistic, I am probably masking. Sometimes I know I am masking and hiding who I really am and other times it just happens.

Hiding who I really am and holding everything in is just so exhausting, because it takes so much effort to do all the things people *expect* – like giving eye contact, joining in with small talk (yuk!), and putting up with sensory stuff. Not being able to talk loads about the things that really matter to me and

having to stop myself stimming is all so draining. It actually hurts me. Stimming can be many things for different people, even fidgeting. Some people jump, flap their hands, tap their feet, jiggle their legs, or rock. It makes me feel really happy when I stim and helps me regulate.

In school other people would make fun of me, especially when I found noises too loud and put my hands over my ears! And wearing noise cancelling headphones wasn't allowed in school, which is just stupid I think, as I really need them loads.

I often find myself putting others first and giving in to things, which is also exhausting for me. I don't always realise that this is what's happening. It is hard for me as I don't want to be mean by saying 'no' to people, but it means I go along with things that maybe I shouldn't.

When I am with friends like Jordan and my new friend that I met at the farm, I feel like I can be me. I don't even need to talk; we just sit and watch stuff or draw and if I get too tired they understand why. I don't feel judged by my friends who are also autistic and I feel like we really connect. "

Jordan

" I didn't realise I masked until I watched something about it online. There was an autistic person talking about what it felt like being in social situations and how they held everything inside. They talked about how when we do this it uses up loads of energy. I could really relate to what they were saying.

As I got a bit older I found any social situation, whether that's school, in church, or with all my family at Christmas, really difficult to cope with. I just felt weird all the time, like I wasn't a normal person. Is there even such a thing as normal anyway? I felt like everyone was watching me all the time and that I had to behave in certain ways to be acceptable and not be seen as weird. I would give eye contact (or else people would keep trying to force me), I would even join in conversations about things that I found boring and pointless, and I would never tell anyone about the things that really interested me.

I now know why so many certain things in school were hard for me, like when everyone has to be completely silent in lessons or exams. I hate total silence! I felt like I just wanted to run out the classroom and escape, but I said nothing and just held it all in. It would have been so helpful if I could have listened to music, but school never would have allowed that. "

CHAPTER 6

Masking

Masking is probably one of the most exhausting experiences for any autistic person and one of the biggest reasons why they experience burnout.

Masking can be something an autistic person is aware of doing, but it's mostly subconscious and is not a choice either. I would also describe it as 'involuntary' – that means it is 'done without will or conscious control'.

Masking can be described as:

- **Camouflaging** – like a chameleon, changing your 'colours' wherever you are.
- **Suppressing** – hiding who you really are and what you really like. Suppressing the pain and distress caused by sensory overload and feeling overwhelmed or exhausted.
- **Adapting/morphing** – changing how you present yourself and what you do, to be acceptable when in certain social environments.
- **Fawning** – people pleasing, going along with things and putting other people and what they need/want

before yourself in order to keep them happy (and stay safe).
- **A trauma response** – just like 'fight/flight/freeze', masking is often a trauma response and is also known as a fear response.

A really well-known autistic advocate and author called Keiran Rose wrote a book about masking with Dr Amy Pearson and they talk about how most autistic masking is due to the stigma there is about autism and being autistic.

So ultimately autistic people mask to stay safe because of stigma. It is important to understand how and when we can unmask and still remain safe.

- **Know that being autistic is not a bad thing** – Learn about your identity and what being autistic really means for you. Know that you are not broken and you do not need to be fixed as a person. You are different and not disordered. Find autistic content creators on social media; learning from other autistic people who are positive about being autistic can be helpful for learning more about yourself.

- **Boundaries with others** – Boundaries are important and keep you safe; I think they are especially important for autistic people to understand. Having boundaries means being able to say 'no' to others and not doing things just to please others.

- **Your neurokin** – Do you know other autistic people like you? Maybe you already have autistic friends who are your 'kin'. Usually it is easier to unmask in environments where there are other autistic people and where there is no stigma and no ableism. There are now more and more online and face-to-face groups for autistic people.

- **Safe places** – I wonder what you think a 'safe' environment is like for you? Do you know the places where you feel free to be you, to be authentically autistic? These are places where you don't feel overwhelmed or overstimulated and where you do not experience sensory overload. They are also places where you can be you, where you can talk about your interests and stim without others asking you to stop or making fun of you for being different.

- **'Should and must' voices** – It is very common for people to have thoughts that are like fixed rules and sound like they 'should, must or have to' be something or do something in a certain way. This can be because of perfectionism and it can lead to a lot of emotional distress and exhaustion. For autistic people it can also lead to masking, because maybe you don't feel ok about being autistic? Maybe you judge yourself and feel you should try to do certain things.

- **Intersectionality** – Intersectionality is a way of understanding that many people have their own individual experiences of discrimination. Lots of things mean a person can end up marginalised – their racial identity, gender, nationality, sexuality, class, physical ability, etc. For many people unmasking is not as easy as just finding safe places for an autistic person to be authentic, it will also need to be safe for them because of race, gender, and sexuality, etc.

Accepting your differences as an autistic person is a process and it's not something that can just happen. Getting to a place where you do things because it is right for you and right for your different needs is better for you and your wellbeing in the long run.

CHAPTER 7

Demands and Expectations

All human beings can find demands difficult at various times, but they can be especially difficult for autistic people and even more so if you are PDA. Everyday demands become really challenging during burnout – demands like looking after yourself (eating, washing, brushing your teeth, dressing) and things like focusing, writing, talking, timekeeping, even things you enjoy doing – so many things become hard and even impossible!

We all have expectations of ourselves and sometimes they might be too high. This might mean you beat yourself up a lot and push yourself too hard. Other people also have expectations of us, whether that is parents, teachers, siblings, family, friends, etc.; they mean well but their expectations of us can also sometimes feel like really heavy weights and demands.

Demands can be all kinds of things:

Internal demands

It's common for autistic people to struggle with perfectionism and this means we find making mistakes really hard; this can make us feel under a lot of pressure. This kind of demand is self-imposed but can often be triggered by other people's expectations or even society's expectations of us as individuals.

Other internal demands might be:

- feelings and emotions (some feelings and emotions can feel difficult to cope with because they might be big and overwhelming sometimes)
- things you want or things you want to do
- choices and decisions
- pain (coping with pain might feel demanding and may mean taking medication)
- hunger and thirst
- feeling bored.

External demands

External demands can be direct, indirect or hidden. A direct demand, for example, is when someone might ask or tell you to do something – a teacher, parent, sibling, etc. Even rewards for something you have done can be direct demands. Often an autistic person might be rewarded for something like giving eye contact or engaging at school by asking or answering a question – when in fact this may have been something they did because they were masking.

An indirect or hidden demand might also be guidelines that you are expected to keep, the expectations there can be to achieve certain standards, and these can come from teachers, parents, other family members, or from society as a whole.

Sometimes people in your life might lower the demands because they understand that is what is best for helping reduce stress, but they still might have certain expectations – perhaps, for example, around education and passing exams. It is important that expectations are seen as demands too and to understand that they can create a lot of pressure.

External demands might also be:

- small talk
- expectations to engage in lessons at school in a certain way
- self-care such as showering, washing your hair, brushing your teeth, etc.
- going to bed to go to sleep
- saying please and thank you
- eating a meal
- homework.

PDA and demands

Some autistic people have what's known as a PDA profile and the best way to describe this is as a 'persistent drive for autonomy'. The official term is 'pathological demand avoidance'.

PDA is not just about resisting or avoiding demands, it's about being wired (by that remember I mean the brain and nervous system) in such a way that the person needs loads of autonomy and to be given *agency* by those around them. When people give you agency they are trusting your capacity to make certain choices and decisions, to have your own thoughts and beliefs, and believe in your ability to do all kinds of things. When a PDAer is not given this agency, they will feel extremely stressed and this can even lead to burnout.

Some of the other characteristics of PDA are:

- may be very sociable but they may be masking their challenges with social situations, communication, and social expectations
- using strategies in social situations such as using humour, pretending, fantasy, and role playing
- often being very focused on other people – real, fictional, or imagined
- very often tend to be creative (common in many neurodivergent people)
- enjoy novelty often, rather than routine or structure (especially if the routine or structure is imposed upon them by others)
- often very determined with a very strong sense of justice and things needing to be equal and fair; do not relate to or see hierarchy (rather they see everyone on an equal footing)
- a very sensitive nervous system with a need for autonomy and a lot of co-regulation with trusted people.

It's not only important for a PDAer to have autonomy and trust, it is essential, and not having autonomy can lead to burnout. Autonomy means 'the ability to make decisions and act without being controlled by anyone else' (Cambridge Dictionary n.d. a) The word autonomy comes from the Greek word 'autonomos' meaning 'self-law' and 'having its own law'.

So this gives you a flavour of why someone who is a PDAer can struggle in environments where there are lots of demands and expectations. In fact, it isn't just hard to cope but it causes a fight, flight, freeze, fawn response in the individual who is PDA, meaning they are likely to be in survival mode all the time – this is also referred to as being hypervigilant.

Demands can be hard for a PDAer, even everyday demands that to others can seem so easy and straightforward. Too many demands can be so debilitating that a PDAer will become exhausted by them and the lack of agency. But masking may mean the individual (and those around them) is unaware of why they are so exhausted and may not realise that the issue is the pressure of all the demands being put upon them.

This all means that for a PDAer certain environments, such as school or college, can be very challenging indeed! In fact there are a very high number of young people with a PDA profile who are not able to attend school. Many of these children are home educated or their families have managed to get an EHCP (Education and Health Care Plan) in the UK or IEP (Individualised Education Plan) in the US and what's known in the UK as an EOTAS package (education other than at school) so they don't have to attend a school setting.

These packages are not easy to get, but for many PDAers it

is the best way forward in regard to education. Of course, not all families are in a position to do this, many parents have to work and so this is why it is so important for schools, colleges, and universities to understand the unique needs of a young person who has a PDA profile, so they do not end up burnt out.

PDA means there is a need for much more flexibility and for things to feel equal and fair. When things are not equal or fair, then a PDAer is likely to experience intense emotions such as high levels of anxiety, stress, and anger too. I have a PDA profile, as does my son. We both understand how important autonomy and fairness is and how important it is to be flexible with each other. We also trust each other a lot and regularly co-regulate, helping each other when we are stressed, anxious, and overwhelmed by people, places, or events.

If you are a teenager, and even if you're not, a fantastic book to help you understand PDA is *The Teen's Guide to PDA* written by Laura Kerbey and illustrated by Eliza Fricker.

CHAPTER 8
Running Out of Energy

One of the most common experiences in burnout is fatigue – a lack of energy. Understanding your energy levels and what has affected them is therefore really important, especially as an autistic person.

Everyone has different kinds of energy: physical, mental, and emotional. Some people just seem to have loads of energy and can do lots of things. Autistic people have differences in their energy levels probably because of the way we process everything more intensely (this is because of being monotropic).

Spoon Theory, developed by Christine Miserandino, can be really helpful when it comes to managing energy levels.

Think of your energy like having a certain number of spoons, everyone has different numbers of spoons. Everything you do, each task, all your social interactions, the places you go to, all use up spoons.

Sometimes by the end of the day all your spoons have been used up and you will have none left for the things you enjoy

that are restful. This can be frustrating when you have lots of ideas and want to do stuff you enjoy doing but are out of spoons. Sometimes it might cause you to push through and risk getting even more exhausted.

Social situations can drain our battery and use up lots of spoons, for example school, college, university, work, shops, family gatherings, etc. Autistic people's experience of environments is much more intense. We are more likely to take in everything around us all at once and this can be really overwhelming and overstimulating. Throw in our sensory and communication differences and we can find things too noisy, too busy, too fast, too stressful, and too overwhelming.

However, the great news is that there are people, places, things, and experiences that can restore our spoons – so think about what things use up your energy and what things restore your energy.

What can help to restore your spoons?

People
There may be people in your life who help restore your spoons rather than draining you. It may be family members,

friends – including online friends. They may be other autistic, neurodivergent people who you connect with.

Places

A walk in nature, a park you like to go to, a historic place, your garden if you have one, or even your bedroom. These are places that can be like an oasis, where you feel free to be quiet or noisy, if that is what you need.

Activities/interests

The things you love the most and maybe think about a lot of the time can be things that restore spoons. Sometimes these are interests that you have for years and some last a short time.

Luna and Jordan: People, Places, and Things That Use Up Spoons

Luna

“Friends and even family use up my spoons. Some people are draining because they communicate loads or because they don't communicate in ways that work for me. Some people just like sending lots and lots of messages, videos, or memes and that can be very demanding for me, because if you're like me I feel I have to answer every single message and that ends up making me very stressed.

Events can be just as bad. I don't really like my birthday much, because my family all want a big party and I hate parties. It's nice that they want to give me presents but then they all want to watch me open them up in front of them all and

> sing to me. I hate everyone looking at me and making me the centre of attention! It takes so much energy to smile and give eye contact and say thank you. I wonder what they will say if I tell them I don't want to go?

Jordan

> Some places use up lots of my spoons, especially when its crowded and there are too many people and too much talking. Often I need to just be on my own, listening to music because I am overwhelmed and overstimulated. My bedroom is my sanctuary as no one disturbs me and my mum, dad, and brother all know to knock before coming in. This is where I go if I need to restore or preserve spoons.

When I was at school, just getting ready in the morning took loads of my spoons. This was mostly because I was absolutely dreading going in! Then once there I would already feel tired and would find it so hard to focus.

All the harsh rules in school are so draining and meant I couldn't even do things that help me to stay calm. So I would get home and have no more spoons for anything I needed to do that could help me as an autistic and ADHD person.

CHAPTER 9
School

Like many autistic young people, both Luna and Jordan experienced burnout and school was a huge part of the reason. Schools, especially secondary or high schools, are mostly really busy, noisy, and demanding environments, where there is a lot of pressure and there are often rigid expectations; there are sometimes a thousand or more other pupils! They are often very different environments to primary or elementary schools.

All the noise, talking, social pressures, constant changing from class to class, and different teachers for each class, can be really exhausting for an autistic pupil. All that plus all the new information you have to take in quickly – which can be very challenging when as an autistic person you process things differently – makes for a really demanding experience.

In recent research a neuroscientist called Dr Sinead Mullally and her team found that out of children not able to attend school in the UK, as many as 83% are autistic and many of them are also ADHD. I think that most of these children and young people are experiencing autistic burnout.

If you are experiencing burnout and you are still on the register at your school, then here is some advice:

- The most important thing is your mental and physical wellbeing – education can be on hold until you are able and feel safe to continue.

- If the school Special Educational Needs Coordinator (SENCo) doesn't understand autistic burnout then it might help them to read this book.

- Recovery involves a lot of rest and you will *need* a significant prolonged break.

- Returning to the school where burnout was triggered is not going to help you. Most young people who experience burnout don't return to their school.

- Education is for life and there are different ways to learn – many autistic people get a place in a more appropriate alternative provision.

- If your family is able to home educate, then many autistic people do very well learning at home. Not all families can do this, though.

Luna and Jordan:
School and Autistic Burnout

Luna

❝When I was in junior school, although I didn't enjoy going much, I had a close friend called Bethany who was also autistic and we used to spend a lot of time together; she helped me loads. Then Bethany had to change schools in Year 6, because she moved to a different area, and I was left on my own. This made going to school much harder.

I tried to play with the other children but kept ending up in arguments and feeling rejected. Teachers started to notice that I seemed very sad and that I had stopped communicating as much as I used to; they talked to my mum, but no one knew how to help me.

Looking back it's so obvious that I am

autistic and yet none of my teachers said anything about autism to my mum. All this has meant that I didn't get a diagnosis till recently!

When I went to secondary school it was like I fell into a really dark hole, it was horrible. I had no friends, the corridors were crowded, noisy, smelly, and everyone stared at me. I found going from lesson to lesson with so many different teachers really hard to cope with and all the different subjects overwhelming and so confusing.

I never felt I belonged and couldn't be myself with anyone. I just tried to push myself to just get through each day, as I was told by teachers that school was important and that not going meant I would never get a job! I don't think that's true but at the time I felt it was.

I don't know how I got through Year 7 and then, in Year 8, I started to experience what I think were probably meltdowns when I got home from school, and it got harder and harder to go in. I started to eat less, stopped talking and messaging friends and felt so tired all the time. I eventually stopped going into school altogether and most days stayed in bed all day. My brain felt like mush.

My mum was really worried and spoke to the school SENCo, and said she thought I was autistic. They told her that school was the best place for me and that she should just get me in every day. But Mum knew that this was not the best thing, as she could see how school was actually exhausting me. Mum did think I might be depressed and asked our doctor to refer me to CAMHS (Child and Adolescent Mental Health Services).

CAMHS eventually wrote to my mum and I was put on their waiting list; I think she felt really helpless. School also put lots of pressure on us and Mum started to get attendance letters, because my attendance got so low, to something like 50%. Mum still didn't make me go in, though, and this was so helpful because I knew I just would not be able to do any lessons, all the constant changes, busy corridors, all the shouting, and other people staring at me all the time. I was just so tired all the time.

Mum applied for an EHCP (Education and Health Care Plan) and, although it was really hard to get, Mum fought hard and we eventually got it. They agreed for me to attend an alternative school that is a bit like a farm. I didn't have the energy to attend at first but after a while I went in for a few hours each week and now I go in a few days each week and love it there! I even get to do horse riding, and I especially love the chickens – I have told Mum I want to keep chickens at home but she's not so keen.

Mum and I now know that what I experienced is autistic burnout and that the best thing for me now that I am feeling better is to be in a quieter environment that doesn't push me so hard and where I can spend time with fewer people – people who are like me, which feels much safer. I don't want to burnout again so I think I will always have to be aware of what the triggers are. 〞

Jordan

❝I was diagnosed autistic when I was 7 and have had an EHCP since junior school. My mum is also autistic. I think my dad is also probably autistic but he doesn't want to get a diagnosis. He just says 'yep, I probably am autistic but I don't need the label'. I don't see being autistic that way – it's not a label.

I have always found school hard even though my junior school was quite small. I never really wanted to go and my mum and dad had to literally drag me there some days – which was horrible! Mum feels really bad that she did this now, but at the time she didn't know what else to do.

I just about managed to get through. What helped me was always wearing my ear defenders and teachers allowing me to have fidget toys, as these helped me focus sometimes. They also realised that I needed movement breaks, as staying still for too long is so hard for me. Then when I was 10 and in Year 6 my mum got me assessed for ADHD.

As soon as I started secondary school, even though we were told it was a school that understood students with the kind of different needs I have, I was not allowed to have a lot of the supports I had in junior school. I felt too self-conscious to wear ear defenders as no one else wore them and I was too scared that I would get bullied; I know now that I was masking a lot. I think I lasted about three months and then just stopped going in. I found all the changes, going from lesson to lesson, so hard and so confusing! I couldn't keep up with all their expectations and all the homework too.

Mum and I talked about me trying another school. We eventually did this and I really tried so hard but it actually felt worse at the new school. Over the next few years I would go into school for a bit and then get exhausted again and not be able to go. Eventually I stopped going to school altogether and I haven't been into school for 18 months now.

In the first year at home I spent most of my time in my bedroom in the dark with my curtains closed, gaming a lot. I couldn't even get dressed most of the time and I was often up all night. ”

CHAPTER 10

The P Word: Puberty and Autistic Burnout

Puberty is something everyone experiences and goes through, I certainly remember it being difficult; it is a time of huge physical, emotional, and mental changes in our brains and bodies. It can be a really tough time for young people and if you are experiencing lots of difficulties at the moment as a young person then puberty may well also be playing a part.

For autistic people there is no doubt that puberty and all the changes play a role in burnout as well as the big transition to secondary school; from a survey that I did, most young autistic people who experience burnout are between 11 and 16 – which tallies with when you are going through puberty and at secondary school.

During puberty there are all kinds of chemical changes taking place within you, massive releases of various hormones such as oestrogen and testosterone that lead to lots of physical transformations. Everything can feel like it is changing and this for an autistic young person can be confusing and upsetting! The experience of puberty is often 'amplified' for an autistic person – this means we can experience it more intensely, whether that is the physical changes in the body, pain and other sensory discomfort, or big emotions. All of this means it can be harder to sleep too.

Puberty is not an easy stage to go through as a young person but it does end – I promise you. For many people things that are really hard in their young teens get easier as they become an older teenager.

There are things that can help practically and emotionally too:

- For people who have periods, like Luna, you may find period pants much easier than pads, which can be very uncomfortable. They are more expensive than normal underwear but can take away the anxiety from worrying about pads falling out. They can be reused, so if you can afford them they will be a good long term investment.

- Some young people find using the contraceptive pill to help control their periods brings them some relief as it can stop them almost completely (for some people it makes them bleed more, so it is best to discuss this with your parents and definitely with a doctor).

- Lots of big emotions can feel horrible and can leave you dysregulated. Your feelings are valid and not wrong. It's really ok to tell someone you trust, even if you don't know what you are feeling/experiencing. Lots of autistic people find emotions really confusing.

    Is there someone, a parent, another family member, a friend (or even a pet) who helps you when you are struggling with big emotions? Co-regulating with another person is something a lot of autistic people find really helpful.

Remember you don't have to tell another person about how you feel by speaking if you can't or don't want to. Maybe message them if talking is hard or impossible.

This book has lots of different ideas to help stay regulated – whether that's because of emotions or sensory overload. I hope some of them can help you.

- It's at this time of your life that you often start to think about who you are, your identity. It's really common for autistic people to identify differently in relation to their sexuality and gender. This is absolutely natural and it's not wrong. It can, however, be a confusing and very difficult time, especially for those people who experience gender dysphoria (distress a person experiences because of a difference between their gender identity and the gender assigned at birth) which can lead to serious mental health issues.

Not everyone is in a situation where they will feel able to discuss this issue with their parents or carers. There are helplines and online services for young people questioning their sexuality or gender and some are mentioned at the end of the book.

Luna and Jordan: Puberty

Luna

❝ When I was little, I hardly noticed my body, but as I got older I started to notice changes that I didn't like. It was so confusing and I found it hard to say out loud what I was going through, because I didn't really know what it was I was feeling! I was changing from a little person into a bigger person.

When it came to gender and identity, this felt really scary too, because people kept saying I was a girl but my mind could not connect with this and it felt wrong to call me a girl or a female. My body was telling me though and that makes me very unhappy some days and maybe even depressed.

I now understand that I am non-binary and this means I don't relate to being female or male. I don't feel like a girl or a boy (and it's different for every non-binary person as some identify as gender fluid or other identities). I am gender non-conforming. I know this is confusing for lots of people, so imagine how confusing "it was for me. But coming out to my mum helped loads as I didn't have to keep it secret anymore. She doesn't completely understand but she is trying to, she respects my pronouns and is doing lots of research too.

I found showering harder and harder as a young teenager, but then I ended up sweaty and smelly. I just wanted my body to stay like it was when I was little, but it just kept on developing, kept on changing. Then came my first period. Oh my God!

I knew it was going to happen at some stage because Mum had spoken to me and we did a lesson in school on periods, but I don't think you can ever really be fully prepared for the discomfort. Mum was brilliant though and got me period pants, which are so much better than wearing big pads that I kept worrying would fall out. I was so scared about leaking in lessons though and would often stay off school if I could because school was not a nice place to be when you are feeling like this."

Jordan

"I used to be really chatty when I was a lot younger but when I turned 11 I noticed that I started to feel more and more self-conscious and started to find that other people, especially other young people, made me feel really anxious. I couldn't talk to them about the things I am really into as they thought I was weird for not enjoying playing sport, for still liking Pokemon, and for not wanting to have a girlfriend.

> I also found that lots of things made me feel really angry and exhausted. I started having more arguments with my little brother; I know it's not his fault but sometimes he is just so annoying!
>
> I get really bad acne too, which really sucks because it means I have to use this special cream; the more my mum asks me to use it the more I don't want to and so the acne hasn't got better, that gets me down some days. I worry about what other people think about my looks and wearing glasses doesn't help either."

CHAPTER 11

When Emotions and Feelings Are Big and Confusing

Emotions can be really confusing things for anyone, but when we go through puberty they can be especially big and messy. For autistic people they can be even more so, as autistic people are more likely to have something called (wait for it, long word coming) alexithymia (alex-ee-thy-mee-a). This word means 'no words for emotions'.

Now let me be clear, this does *not* mean that autistic people do not have emotions; autistic people are human and just like every other human we have emotions. However, about 55% or more of autistic people find it hard to identify and describe their emotions and therefore find it harder to understand, explain, and communicate their emotions to others. They might also find other people's emotions a bit confusing.

It's important to know that autistic people can have loads of empathy, despite many believing that they don't. 'Empathy is the ability to understand and appreciate another person's feelings and experience' (Faculty of Philosophy, University of Oxford n.d.).

Not understanding your emotions does not mean you don't have empathy. In fact, autistic people are usually really caring and very concerned about things that happen to others; they can feel a very strong need for justice and fairness. I often experience very strong emotions about various situations that I feel are unjust – to the point where it can be overwhelming.

Not being able to identify what is happening within you emotionally does have a real downside, as it can mean your emotions become dysregulated. Being regulated is all about balance and about being able to apply the brakes and turn things like big emotions down – a bit like what you do with a dimmer switch that turns the light levels up and down according to what is most comfortable.

If you don't know what emotions you are experiencing, you might not know you need to do something about it and may also not know how. This could mean you feel overwhelmed and as though you have a big ball of different emotions inside you. There are things that can help with alexithymia and interoception differences (interoception is the sense we all have of our body's internal signals, such as hunger, thirst, emotions, pain, etc.).

Some autistic people get help from what are known as somatic coaches – these are trained people who help you to understand your nervous system and what it is like to feel safe (sensory and emotional). Some autistic people see occupational therapists who understand the autistic sensory experience and know what is helpful for a neurodivergent person.

Autistic people can experience anxiety a lot, but being autistic is *not* why an autistic person is anxious. The anxiety an autistic person might experience is usually because of the environments they are in. Someone who talks about this a lot is Dr Luke Beardon, who says that 'Autism plus environment = outcome'.

What he means by this is that it can be the environment where an autistic person is in that leads to things like anxiety – that might be school, college, university, hospital, work, or home environments. These environments may cause sensory overload, there might be too many demands, and they might not feel like safe places where an autistic person can be authentic.

Sometimes anxiety is better described as 'dread', and this is because an autistic person usually *knows* that a certain place or situation, for example, is going to be stressful, overwhelming, and exhausting.

What things might help you to regulate emotions?

Talking/communicating

Talking is not the only way to communicate; some autistic people do not talk and some do not talk in certain situations. Communicating with someone who is trustworthy about the things you are struggling with is a really important way to stay safe. Telling someone who listens is a really great way to help you regulate, as sometimes they can see things that we cannot. Sometimes another person might be able to empathise and help you reframe something that has upset you if needed. It is always important that you know your emotions are not wrong and that no one makes you feel this way.

Sometimes talking to a counsellor is a really good way to look at your emotions and things you are struggling with. It is best to find a counsellor who is 'neuro affirming' – this should mean that they accept and understand autism, masking, sensory needs, etc., sometimes from lived experience. Not all types of therapy or counselling are helpful for an autistic person, as some therapies try to make autistic people comply with neurotypical ways of being rather than accept themselves as a neurodivergent person (something called applied behavioural analysis can be seen as doing this).

Cognitive behavioural therapy (CBT) is also often not recommended because of the differences in how an autistic person processes thoughts and feelings and also because a CBT practitioner may sometimes use exposure therapy. Exposure therapy seeks to help a person build resilience in various situations that cause anxiety. This could mean an autistic person is encouraged to remain in an environment or situation that is actually causing them harm, such as sensory overload, and could very likely lead to masking.

Counselling might not be appropriate during burnout as talking can be exhausting. Once you have energy it might be something to consider.

Co-regulating with another person
Lots of us have family members or friends we trust who help us by just being there or by doing certain things together.

Maybe you have a parent or carer who helps you by just sitting with you, watching something with you, or joining in with your interests. My son and I do this by watching things we both enjoy together – we might binge watch a Netflix series like *The Umbrella Academy* or *Stranger Things*. Just being together and connecting is often enough.

We also stim together, making silly noises or speaking with different regional accents, which often means we end up in stitches.

Listening to music
Music is a very powerful way to regulate for a lot of people, as we can often match our feelings with different pieces of music or listen to particular songs that helps us think of happy things, certain memories, or places. Some songs can help us to express emotions; I don't know about you but certain songs make me cry and sometimes that is exactly what we need to do.

Going for a walk
Movement can be really important in regulation, as it releases certain chemicals into our body, like dopamine, endorphins, and serotonin, which help us to regulate and feel more settled. You can walk with others or on your own (as long as you are safe and not putting yourself in danger). A walk around the block, a walk in a park or in nature can help you to dim any intense emotions and bring some balance to your thoughts too.

Gaming
Lots of autistic people find gaming helps them regulate. Jordan spends a lot of time gaming, it also helps him

connect with some of his friends. When he is gaming his monotropic brain becomes so intensely focused that everything else goes out of focus, it's like he disappears and all that matters is Jordan and the game.

Interests

Intense interests (which might also be gaming) can really help with regulation and so spending lots of unrestricted time with interests and passions is important and can even help you sleep better. Both Jordan and Luna's interests (music, reading, art, *Stranger Things*, etc.) not only bring them a lot of happiness but also helps their brains not to feel so busy and overwhelmed.

Pets

Dogs, cats, rabbits, snakes, geckos, chickens even, whatever the pet, for many autistic people they are an essential way to connect, regulate, and feel calmer. Pets give unconditional love and affection and are often not demanding (well not always!).

Stimming

Every human does this, whether they know it or not. It can include tapping fingers or feet, cracking knuckles, fidgeting, biting nails, pacing, rocking, jumping, bouncing, swaying, humming, singing. Stimming can be all kinds of repetitive behaviours that bring joy and comfort, help us regulate ourselves, and even help with focus.

Autistic people can stim a lot and it is never wrong, but sometimes certain stims might lead to some level of physical harm. These are known as self-injurious stims and might need to be replaced with something that doesn't lead to harm.

Laughing
Watch a funny film or a video clip. Lots of people enjoy watching short clips on Instagram of cats doing silly things or people having unfortunate accidents. Laughing is a wonderful way to co-regulate with other people too.

Singing
Yes, singing! And even humming too. Your vagus nerve is connected to your vocal cords, so singing and humming are a great way to regulate. The vagus nerve (vagus means 'wanderer') is a huge nerve that is part of what's known as the parasympathetic nervous system and is responsible for helping us to feel safe within ourselves and not in fight or flight. Lots of stims activate the vagus nerve.

Deep breathing
Maybe you know about this and do deep breathing already (although some people don't like it as it can make them feel a bit odd). Deep and slow breaths in and out can be very effective as a way of regulating.

Please note that rapid breathing techniques can actually release more stress chemicals such as cortisol and adrenaline. This will make a person more dysregulated if they are already very stressed.

Visualisations
Sometimes people do deep breathing whilst imagining safe places in their mind. These are called visualisations. They think of a safe place, either imagined or a real place they have been. Maybe have a go? I often think about beautiful places that I have been to and imagine myself walking around and taking in the surroundings.

CHAPTER 12

All Our Different Senses

One of the other big reasons for autistic people experiencing burnout is sensory overload. So understanding the senses and your experience of them is important. People say we have five senses: touch, sound, smell, taste, and sight. But actually we have a lot more – at least nine (I include neuroception, which is our sense of danger and safety). One of the important things to understand about our sensory system is that each autistic person experiences their senses differently – they might be over (hyper)sensitive or under (hypo)sensitive and this can be different for each of their many senses.

For example, Luna is hypersensitive to sudden loud noises that can cause them to feel distressed, so they avoid places where this might happen as much as possible and wear noise cancelling headphones. They also use fidget toys to help feel more regulated in social situations and their stims are usually rocking, tapping the tips of their fingers together, and singing. Luna really enjoys tight hugs with their mum, eating spicy curries, and taking long, warm showers.

Jordan also finds certain sudden noises really hard to

cope with but enjoys really loud music and almost always wears his headphones. Jordan's stims are flapping his hands, biting his fingernails and when he was little he loved jumping on his trampoline and would often spend hours on there just bouncing. He doesn't, however, like a lot of food textures, especially vegetables, and prefers foods that are quite plain and don't have strong flavours. Jordan doesn't like touch and avoids hugs because they hurt.

Here are some of those other senses that you might not have heard of, because they are talked about less commonly.

Proprioception (pro-prio-sep-shun) is the sense of your body's movement, force, heaviness (your limbs for example), and where your body is positioned.

Vestibular (vest-tib-u-lar) is closely linked to proprioception and is the sense of movement and balance.

Interoception (in-tero-sep-shun) is a really important sense to understand, as it's how we get the signals from our body about things like hunger, thirst, pain, needing the toilet, emotions and feelings, and lots of other things. If a person has undersensitive interoception (sometimes referred to as muted) they might not know they are thirsty and get dehydrated, or not know they are in pain and so not seek help. But a person can also be hypersensitive and experience certain signals strongly; for example, I can often really feel my heartbeat and I am also very sensitive to pain.

Interoception and being monotropic (remember autistic brains are monotropic and are focused more intensely on fewer things) kind of go hand in hand, because when we get intensely focused on something we can find we don't get those interoceptive signals. How many times have you been really engrossed in something and forgotten to drink water or haven't realised that you were hungry?

Neuroception (new-row-sep-shun) is everything to do with the sense of safety and danger. Remember we talked about the different fear responses (fight, flight, freeze, fawn, flop) earlier in the book. Autistic people's brains and nervous systems are more sensitive to things that are experienced as a threat. The things that trigger a fear response in an autistic person might be different to someone who is not autistic, because of things like our sensory system differences.

What can help an autistic person with their senses?

Here are a few ideas of things that can help with sensory overload and sensory seeking.

Noise cancelling headphones
These can be a life saver for autistic people! They can be very expensive but you don't need a brand new pair, you can buy them second hand too. Being able to block out or reduce certain noises in various environments can mean the difference between feeling calm and being dysregulated.

Fidget toys and tools
I am 56 years old and I use something called therapy putty and other fidget toys, so try to not see these as just for little kids. Fidgets are often small, and you can pop them in a

pocket or in your bag and they are there for when you might need them.

Weighted blankets

Many autistic people can find physical pressure and weight helpful and this is where weighted blankets can be a great idea. Weighted blankets are just as they sound: soft blankets with weights sewn into them to make them heavier. There are even weighted clothes (mind you they are quite expensive!). Weighted blankets need to be a certain weight compared to the person in order to be really effective, so it's always best to order one from a reputable store so that you get the one that is right for you.

Music

Music is a universal language and it can have a powerful effect upon us. I haven't met a single person who didn't like some sort of music. Listening to music can comfort us and lift us up when we feel sad. It can motivate us and help regulate us. Sometimes certain songs are like old friends that understand what we are experiencing.

Accommodations and adjustments

An accommodation means adjusting or adapting *something* or *somewhere* in order to make it more accessible for people. For autistic people this might mean making somewhere quieter, less busy, changing the lighting, or making sure plans have more structure. It might also mean a group that has been specifically created for autistic and other neurodivergent people to get together.

Stimming

I have talked about this in the previous chapter. Stimming

can help when you are feeling overwhelmed and can help you when you are experiencing or prevent you from experiencing sensory overload. Stimming can also be sensory seeking and can help satisfy a craving for sensory input and regulation.

Safe foods
It is really common for autistic people to find certain foods difficult to eat because of the texture, taste, smell, appearance, etc. Safe foods are foods that we don't struggle to eat that may also help to comfort us – they might even be chewy, spicy, or crunchy and the effect of eating these foods is enjoyable.

Hugging something or someone
Whether it's a pet, a person, or a soft toy, the act of hugging can be really calming for some people. It can make you feel connected and can release feel good chemicals such as dopamine and serotonin that bring joy and regulation.

Luna and Jordan:
Emotional and Sensory Overload

Luna

> If I tell you that sometimes sudden loud noises are so horrible that I can feel really panicky, you might feel the same way? I can really struggle with sensory overload and that can mean things like loud noises, bright flickering lights, yukky, slimy textures, strong smells, and loads of other things are regularly difficult for me. Sensory overload is horrible and can lead to meltdowns. Meltdowns are not tantrums as lots of people think. It's like they happen 'to me' and although I can hold them in for so long they eventually happen.
>
> I don't always know what the feeling is that I am experiencing when things are too loud or bright, but it isn't nice. I think sensory

overload probably makes me really anxious – that's what my mum tells me it is. I think she's right.

When I go to busy places that I know will be noisy, I always take my noise cancelling headphones, as without them I might end up wanting to leave. I used to be worried about what others think of me but recently I have decided that it's ok and I don't care what people think – well, most of the time, anyway.

It is hard for autistic people like me when there are other people around as they are unpredictable and I don't like unpredictability! I also don't feel able to always just be me. I feel like everyone is just staring at me and thinking I am weird because I am stimming and because I have fidget toys to help me. It's ok when I am with my other autistic friends though, as they are like me and get it.

Being in school all day with all the other people, teachers speaking, noisy corridors, people laughing, screaming, shouting, and bells ringing, I would feel like my whole body was going to explode. When I got home I would often end up in a meltdown – like I was a bottle of Pepsi that had been shaken all day and then the lid comes off at home and explodes!

My meltdowns don't last long but it takes me a long time to feel ok again; I feel really tired afterwards. Mum was always great with me in a meltdown and would just sit next to me and stay quiet whilst I would scream. She didn't try to chat, ask any questions or try to ask if I was ok, because it is obvious I am not when I am in a meltdown. 〞

Jordan

❝ Sometimes I can feel really sad inside and sometimes I feel angry, like I am going to explode! But I don't know how I got there. I didn't wake up angry so how come it happens? I read in a book that anger is not the first emotion we feel, but that there are other emotions we feel before anger. But I don't seem to be able to recognise these or figure it all out and it has meant I have ended up in meltdowns. I feel really bad when that happens and all the emotions I feel inside me get big and really confusing.

If my parents try to talk to me when I am feeling like this, I can get really stuck and words won't come out. It's best they just let me feel what I am feeling, rather than try to fix it. One thing that I have learned to do is to scream into my pillow and even punch it! It's like I need to get it all out. I also find listening to music helps me loads. 〞

PART III
RECOVERY, PREVENTION, AND LOOKING AHEAD

CHAPTER 13

Recovery and Prevention

A lot of the things suggested in this section are to help with recovery from autistic burnout but they will also help you with preventing burnout. Recovery isn't just about feeling better again but also about living in a way that is more sustainable for you as an autistic person, so you don't end up always just surviving and never thriving.

Going through autistic burnout can be really difficult and it is important that you don't push yourself or rush to feel better. It is also important that no one else pushes you as rushing recovery can mean you might become exhausted again. Understanding your energy levels and what affects your capacity is important in both the recovery and the prevention of burnout – (remember what we said about spoons?).

When I have spoken to other autistic people, including lots

of young people, they have all said that what was really important was lowering demands, taking time out of education, and resting loads.

What rest means

Rest doesn't just mean sleep. All sorts of things count as rest and can help you get out of survival mode. You need a lot of physical rest but also:

- **Creative** rest – by spending time with your interests and passions when you can.
- **Emotional** rest – by spending time doing things that help you feel good about yourself and help you regulate.
- **Mental** rest – by not pushing yourself or making too many decisions or plans.
- **Social** rest – connecting with others who are also autistic is important but during burnout you may need more time alone in order to feel safe.

Rest also means:

Reducing demands
This is important for you to understand and for all the adults in your life to know about too. Too many demands and expectations can be really unhelpful for an autistic person and especially when you are recovering from burnout.

Conserving energy
In burnout, especially, autistic people can feel very low in

energy. Remember we looked at spoons in relation to energy? Keep an eye on how many spoons you use up in a day (your capacity) as this is a way to help you in recovery and to also prevent burnout going forward.

Sensory needs
It can be helpful to think of our sensory needs a bit like a diet. There is sensory input that we need (that leads to sensory seeking) and there are things that we need others to adjust or things we need to avoid – because they lead to sensory overload.

Time
You cannot rush recovery, it takes time. There is no set time; it is different for every autistic person. If you can, try to take a day at a time, as this can be really helpful. I know that is not always easy as there are lots of expectations from others and society (even your own expectations of yourself) that can put you under a lot of pressure to feel better quickly. To help with recovery and prevent burnout happening again you can learn to pace yourself.

The recovery journey

Recovery is a journey and not a destination and it can take time – this is different for everyone. From a place of being exhausted and crashing, you may (as I discussed earlier) experience a need to hibernate and prefer being nocturnal. This is not an easy part of the recovery journey but you will eventually feel able to do more, as you allow yourself to rest. Do not push yourself (or let others push you, as much as you can). Rest involves time with interests – whatever that may

RECOVERY AND PREVENTION

be: gaming, drawing, writing, reading, nature, Taylor Swift, *Stranger Things*, Lego, history.

Eventually you will emerge from hibernation as your nervous system heals and start to feel safer. What you do then to stay in a place of recovery is crucial as going back to environments that are triggering and not right for you and your neurology may mean you experience burnout again.

What might 'safe' look and feel like?

Emerging out of a place of survival into a place where you feel safer in your mind and your body might look and feel very different for every autistic young person. For example:

- You might have more spoons (energy) for things generally.
- You might be more able to do some of the things you really enjoy doing.
- You might have more energy for seeing other people.
- You might feel more able to go out and about on short trips, walks, etc.
- You might be able to communicate more.
- You might notice that your mind is quieter and not so noisy with racing thoughts.
- You might feel less confused and more able to make decisions and plans.
- You might not have too many demands and expectations to deal with and find that you have more autonomy.

Remember 'safe' means you are not in survival mode (with a fight, flight, freeze, fawn response) all the time. For many people it can mean being more regulated, being themselves, connecting with others, and feeling like they belong.

What else helps recovery?

Be very kind to yourself
Many autistic young people can struggle with their self-worth and might be hard on themselves for experiencing

burnout. By resting you are not doing anything wrong. Be kind and compassionate towards yourself, eat your safe foods, rest loads, snuggle watching your favourite shows, and enjoy any glimmers you find (I explain glimmers below).

Embrace your amazing brain
Both Luna and Jordan have found it helpful as autistic young people to accept and embrace their differences. They are learning more and more about what helps them and what is harmful for their different brains and nervous systems.

Neurokin
Other autistic friends, often called neurokin, can be essential for autistic people. Because lots of environments are not inclusive, this can mean an autistic person can end up masking, so it can be safer to be around other autistic people. Jordan and Luna are good friends and enjoy just being together unmasked, sharing interests, and things that are important to them.

Time with your interests
Remember your interests are more than just hobbies, they are really important for your wellbeing – even if they don't last very long. Your brain is wired to focus intensely on fewer things and spending time with those things is a way of resting and regulating.

Boundaries
Boundaries are really important – as they can help to keep you safe and that includes your energy levels. There are different kinds of boundaries for different types of situations. A boundary is like drawing a line and when someone

crosses that line then it is not ok. You may need help in understanding what those lines are regarding:

- your body
- your money
- your time
- your energy
- your emotions
- your wellbeing and mental health.

Saying 'No' is a really important life skill and it is ok to say it, especially when you think something is not safe for you and your wellbeing, for example, if you know something or someone will harm you, disrespect you, take advantage of you, or use up precious energy.

Sometimes we might need someone else to help us with asserting ourselves and setting boundaries with others – it can be hard to say 'No'. As an autistic person it is also important to understand when masking might mean you might find identifying and holding boundaries harder.

Glimmers
Glimmers are the opposite to triggers – they are little moments of joy or micro-moments that can soothe you, boost your mental health, and help your nervous system feel safer.

Glimmers might be seeing a beautiful sunset, the moon, a rainbow, or something else in nature, looking at a collection you have and enjoying all the colours or how they are arranged and organised; a sensory moment of joy such as crunching leaves or acorns as you walk; eating food you enjoy and so many other things.

Luna and Jordan:
Recovery

Luna

❝I have realised recently that I have been struggling with burnout for ages, probably daily sometimes, since I was little. I would get home from school and flop on the sofa, not able to do my homework. Even in Year 6 I would get home and then it was like I would burst and everything that had built up in school would explode. I expect puberty might not have helped either. I hated it when I started my periods, I felt really paranoid and anxious a lot of the time. It's still horrible.

I needed the time I had at home away from what felt like chaos. There were too many demands and pressure; I couldn't think because I was just so exhausted. I never felt safe at school other than when I was with my friend who is still there. She comes to my house sometimes and we watch things and do drawing together. I also chat with Jordan on Instagram loads.

It has taken a long time, but I have just started going to a new school that isn't like school at all actually.

> It's like a farm and there are people who I guess are sort of like teachers, but we don't have lessons in the same way as in my old school. If I have days when I can't go in, they are really kind and allow me time to get my energy back again. I love it there! They know I can find talking hard and that some days I might find any communication exhausting but they don't push me, which is really important. Recovery for me is not about going back to how things were or else I will just burn out again.

Jordan

> I don't think I am the same person that I was before I started to feel exhausted and burnt out. I have realised that I was masking so much, and that I had been for a very long time, especially in school. Being at home and spending lots of time in my room hasn't always been a nice experience but I am starting to spend more time with my family again.
>
> There are a few things about school that I miss, such as some of my friends and even one of my teachers who was very kind to me. I can't go back to school though and so at the moment my education is on hold.
>
> With the support of my mum and dad and even my friend Luna I have been able to stop everything that was using up all my energy. I have to be careful as sometimes my head tells me I can do loads and I push myself. This can exhaust me. Also, because I am autistic and ADHD my head gets really busy with all kinds of

thoughts racing around like bees; I hate that. So my mum is looking at medication for ADHD to see if that will help me because I didn't want to try it when I was first diagnosed.

I still have days when I am really tired, but I hope I will start to be able to go out more; there is no rush. Mum tells me that the most important thing is feeling safe in my mind and my body. I know I am very lucky to have her as she understands. There are other members of our family who haven't always agreed with Mum and Dad letting me rest at home and I have heard Mum talking to my granny about how school is not a helpful place for me. It can be hard for other people to understand autistic burnout.

I don't want to ever feel like I did when I was in full burnout. I would like to find ways and have the right support so that it won't happen and if I do start to feel it is happening again I will know what to do. 〃

CHAPTER 14
Stories of Hope

I hope this book has helped you understand what autistic burnout is and what might cause it, so that you can look after yourself and ask other people for help to stay safe and well.

Before we end, I wanted to share lived experience examples of young people like you, who have experienced autistic burnout and are on recovery journeys. Hope is such a powerful force and can be the very thing that can help us get through a difficult situation. When we are feeling unwell, sad, hopeless, etc. and we project how we feel into the future, this can mean we don't have hope. We might think that everything is just going to remain as it is at this moment. But things can and do change.

If everything seems dark, it can be hard to find light. This is why taking a day at a time is so important. This moment might seem awful and you may be wondering if it will ever change, but I want to encourage you – it really can change; it might take time, but it will change. There is a light at the end of what can feel like a very long tunnel.

Liv's story

"I am Liv, I am aged 14 and live with my mum who is also autistic. I was diagnosed as autistic in 2022. I am probably PDA and ADHD too.

My transition from primary to secondary school was different due to Covid lockdowns and we were in small classroom bubbles. I found getting back to the full-time timetable so hard to cope with. I started to find certain lessons harder than others, I didn't want to join in, and this even led to threats of me being sent to the exclusion area. The school staff did not understand me or why I was upset about things but instead called me rude and defiant!

I started to find it harder and harder to attend school; I felt so tired. I just wanted to stay in bed all day, every day. It was so difficult for me to focus on lessons and schoolwork and I became even more sensitive to noise and touch. I started getting more and more headaches all the time and Mum thought that something might be wrong with my eyesight. I started to eat more and then on other days I couldn't eat anything at all. On the days when I felt anxious I just wanted my 'safe' foods and 'safe' clothes. I also stopped doing all the things I had previously enjoyed – scouts, archery, and seeing friends.

Just the thought of going into school would lead to me vomiting, as I was so anxious and worried. I would think about the teachers I didn't like, the crowded corridors, the constant sudden changes, and all those other young people in the building. Mum would try to get me up and ready to go in, as we were told I had to be in school, but I would just lie there motionless, shutdown, unable to communicate, my curtains closed.

The turning point was the day that my mum tried and tried to get me out of bed and I ended up hiding under my desk, completely overwhelmed! I was exhausted and that exhaustion was all consuming.

My mum sought advice and found out that what I was experiencing was called autistic burnout. She realised that school was not somewhere that I was able to be and together we looked at what was going to help me feel better again. Not being at school really helped, but this doesn't mean I don't want to learn new things, as I love learning. I was, however, scared that Mum might suddenly say that I had to go back and this caused me a lot of anxiety. She didn't, though, and together we have looked at what works for me as an autistic person.

It has taken me a few years to get to a place of feeling more myself. I am not exhausted all the time. I still get tired in social situations, though, and I have to manage those times spent where there are other people. I am learning about masking but it is so hard to not mask when you have done it for so long."

M's story

"What I find helpful when I am in burnout and as a way to reduce burnout is recognising that at some times it's not helpful for me to speak for a long time, or at all.

If I'm already low on spoons, I sometimes decide to either not talk about what I'm currently interested in or try to give a truncated version. This is because when I'm excited about something I can be very energetic and talk for a long time, and then I suddenly hit a wall and just feel completely drained.

If it feels like an invisible force is keeping my mouth shut I sometimes try to say or sing something to see if it dispels and, if it gets worse, I tell myself that today the sense that needs a break is talking and that's ok – if I need to communicate I can either gesture to things or write them down and show people.

The main thing is that I find it helpful to have, if possible, at least a day of being able to do pretty much nothing either side of a day where I have to do lots of things/one big thing.

For example, I have choir every Monday, which I really enjoy, and it's two and a half hours long. But it's not just choir, it's all the getting ready beforehand which in and of itself can take a lot of energy, the transport, etc. etc. I've sacrificed some things at the moment in order for me to have the capacity to both enjoy my time there and not be too drained later in the week.

If I go to church on a Sunday I might not have as much in me to go to choir, and I really enjoy choir. It also means that I don't often make it to small group because that meets on a Tuesday. It's sad in a way, but I kind of have to choose what to prioritise because I used to go to most if not all of the events/meetings that

> I wanted to, and looking back I don't think that was sustainable for me.
>
> What I'm really blessed to have is people who understand that I might not always have the capacity to see or talk to them, but are happy when I do. That means I can still have community, but with less pressure.
>
> In short what helps is:
>
> 1. Talking less, if at all.
> 2. Prioritising what to go to in a week and having lots of rest either side of activities/chores.
> 3. An understanding community.

Josh's story

> I think burnout started for me when I was 10/11 and in Year 6; I remember feeling really low all the time and I didn't really understand why.
>
> Secondary school was especially difficult because I was introduced to a completely new environment that was big and loud, and bullies would see my suffering as an opportunity to tease me. I was also patronised and infantilised a lot by teachers and found myself masking in order to avoid this as much as possible. The expectations and pressure put on me to 'push on' and 'be resilient' only exhausted me even more and so I spent a lot of days, sometimes weeks, at home.
>
> My mum never pressured me to go to school when I

couldn't, which I'm very grateful for. I spent a lot of days lying down, playing games and watching YouTube, Twitch, or my favourite TV shows, because they helped me to regulate and take my mind off school. I often beat myself up because I felt that I was being 'lazy', but I absolutely wasn't – I was burnt out and needed to rest.

When I finished secondary school I went to college. I spent four months there and then dropped out, because of how traumatic and exhausting I found it. People then asked me what I was planning to do next, but I didn't have a plan; I didn't want to do anything except to be at home looking after my mental health.

It's been over a year since then and I feel so much happier now; I wouldn't say I've fully recovered, but I definitely feel like I have more energy to do things! "

Anonymous's story

" Burnout has completely altered the person I could have been. The school system played a large role in that, with its rigid curriculum, restricting the creative side of me which I need to function. I have been in burnout because of a broken system for over two years at this point. For me this meant I could not focus properly and was in a constant state of fatigue, resulting in so-called academic decline, which left me feeling devastated and incompetent.

I was consistently told by authoritative figures that this was the only way to be, and I must seek out therapies like CBT and ABA as there was no way their 'perfect system' could cause these symptoms. These people were supposed to be educated on special educational needs and disabilities (SEND) too – instead what they were recommending overwhelmed me to the point of exhaustion and school absence.

School coded me into thinking like a progress bar; every time I was praised or congratulated the bar would fill, with promise of a 'reward' at the end – no matter how gruelling or minuscule the task. For me, the reward never came. It frustrates me beyond belief that this is allowed to continue and to harm neurodivergent students like myself.

In my recovery I have started to play through my favourite video games and collect all the achievements. These tasks may seem small to many, yet I can feel myself healing with every piece of progress made. I have also turned to advocacy and writing to try and pace myself out of burnout, and I am still learning coping mechanisms to accompany this.

I am slowly gaining confidence and find myself recovering, even if it is 0.1% per month. So, to those who are stuck, my advice would be to keep believing in yourself and find your passions. Best of luck out there. ”

Helpful Books and Websites

For understanding autism and ADHD
- Autism Understood: https://autismunderstood.co.uk
- Neurodivergent Lou: on Facebook and Instagram
- Autistic Callum: on Facebook and Instagram

For understanding PDA
- Laura Kerbey and Eliza Fricker (2024) *The Teens Guide to PDA*, Jessica Kingsley Publishers.
- Laura Hellfeld: https://laurahellfeld.co.uk

LGBTQIA
- Yenn Purkis (2022) *The Awesome Autistic Guide for Trans Teens*, Jessica Kingsley Publishers.
- Yenn Purkis and Wenn Lawson (2021) *The Autistic Trans Guide to Life*, Jessica Kingsley Publishers.
- LGBTQIA Helpline: https://switchboard.lgbt
- Stonewall: www.stonewall.org.uk/young-futures

Mental health websites
- Papyrus: www.papyrus-uk.org
- Young Minds: www.youngminds.org.uk
- The Mix: www.themix.org.uk

Some of the co-occurring conditions mentioned in the book
- HSD (hypermobility): www.ehlers-danlos.com/what-is-hsd
- EDS (Ehlers-Danos syndrome): www.sedsconnective.org
- PoTS (postural orthostatic tachycardia syndrome): www.potsuk.org

Glossary

Here are some words that you will find in this book and their explanation (and some other words not in the book that you might find it useful to understand the meaning of).

ADHD A different neurotype (type of brain). Approximately 50–80% of autistic people are also ADHD. An ADHD brain has all kinds of differences including levels of certain hormones such as noradrenaline, dopamine, and gamma-aminobutyric acid (GABA). Some people who are ADHD find medication can be helpful with executive function differences (focus, starting tasks, impulsivity, planning, emotional regulation, decision making, working memory, etc.). A person who is autistic and ADHD is known as 'AuDHD'.

Alexithymia (alex-ee-thy-mee-a) This means 'having no words for emotions' and 50% or more of autistic people have alexithymia. It does not mean they don't have emotions, but it does mean they can struggle to recognise, explain, and express their emotions and can mean it is harder to interpret and understand the emotions of other people.

Autism A different neurotype (type of brain). It is not something a person lives with, or a disorder, but a different way of seeing, feeling, and experiencing the world. An autistic person has different sensory, communication, social, and executive functioning needs. Autistic people are not high or low functioning, but all have different strengths, challenges, and different needs.

Autistic inertia It is common for autistic people to sometimes find it hard to start things (task initiation), change focus, and finish things. This is linked to being monotropic and probably due to executive functioning differences.

Double empathy problem Autistic people can find it exhausting and confusing to understand non-autistic ways of communicating. Likewise, non-autistic people might feel uncomfortable when they are around autistic people because their usual ways of communicating do not work as well.

This mismatch between social expectations and experiences can make communication between autistic and non-autistic people difficult. That is why building understanding and empathy is described as a 'double problem', because both autistic and non-autistic people struggle to understand each other (Crompton *et al.* 2021).

Echolalia Noises and sounds made which can be: words, accents, impersonations, singing, and even just noises that might be repeated. It's also thought of as vocal stimming. The word echolalia comes from the Greek words 'echo' and 'lalia' and this means 'to repeat speech'.

Executive function Any of the cognitive (thinking and reasoning) functions that take place in the prefrontal cortex of the brain and include:

- decision making
- emotional regulation
- flexibility
- focus
- impulse control/self-control
- organising skills
- planning and prioritising things
- reflection upon self and actions
- stress tolerance
- task initiation
- time management
- working memory.

Identity first language Most autistic people prefer saying they are autistic (rather than a person with autism), as autistic people cannot be separated from their identity. This is the most validating language to use.

Interoception This is part of the sensory system that helps us to perceive internal signals, whether that is breathing, our heartbeat, pain, emotions, or things like hunger, thirst, and knowing we need the toilet. Interoception, like any of our other senses, can be muted (undersensitive) or heightened (oversensitive).

Medical (deficit) model The outdated and the most dominant model of understanding what autism is, based upon concepts and theories dating back many years.

Meltdowns (fight/flight) It's important to stress that meltdowns are not tantrums but happen because an autistic person is very distressed and overwhelmed. Meltdowns are involuntary and triggered by stress and many other things. The person is in a state of what is known as hyperarousal.

Monotropism Autistic brains are more likely to be monotropic, which means they are pulled in more intensely, more strongly, towards one or several interests. Constantly changing focus and not being able to hyperfocus on interests can be debilitating.

Hyperfocusing can lead to what is called a 'flow state' and can help an autistic person regulate and be very productive. Monotropism is a theory that helps us understand autistic brains that was developed by autistic people, initially by Dinah Murray, Mike Lesser, and Wenn Lawson in 2005.

Neurodivergent 'Sometimes abbreviated to ND, it means having a mind that functions in ways which diverge significantly from the dominant societal standards of "normal"' (Walker n.d.).

Neurodiverse 'A group of people is neurodiverse if one or more members of the group differ substantially from other members in terms of their neurocognitive functioning' (Walker n.d.).

Neurodiversity 'The diversity of human minds, the infinite variation in neurocognitive functioning within humans' (Walker n.d.).

Neurotypical 'Often abbreviated to NT, it means having a style of neurocognitive functioning that falls within the dominant societal standards of "normal"' (Walker n.d.).

OCD 17–37% of autistic young people also have obsessive compulsive disorder (OCD). OCD includes having recurring intrusive thoughts and repetitive behaviours, also known as rituals, that the person cannot control. These repetitive behaviours are unwanted and can be harmful.

PDA Pathological demand avoidance, also known as a *persistent drive for autonomy*. An autistic person might have a PDA profile. A person who is PDA can find all kinds of demands very challenging and may go to considerable lengths to avoid them. They need a lot of autonomy and can experience very high levels of anxiety due to the amount of demands and expectations there can be.

Person first language This comes from the belief that the individual is separate from autism. This is the language preferred by professionals but most autistic people feel that this language is invalidating and unhelpful.

Sensory needs Our senses include:

- sight, hearing, taste, touch, smell
- interoception (internal signals from body)
- vestibular (movement and balance)
- proprioception (sense of where body is in space)
- neuroception (sense of safety/threat).

Autistic people can be hypo (under) or hyper (over)sensitive to different senses.

Shutdowns (freeze) These can be triggered by very similar things to meltdowns and may also happen after meltdowns. They are involuntary and the person is not attention seeking or being difficult. The person is in a state of hypo-arousal.

Social model This is a movement that celebrates, respects, and sees autistic people and their individual needs; it seeks to remove the barriers that there are in society that lead to stigmatisation and ableism.

Special interest and passions These are not obsessions but are strong, sometimes intense interests that an autistic person might well hyperfocus upon, sometimes for a long time. These can change but some may last their whole life.

Stimming This is something all humans do and is often physical movement of some kind that can help a person to regulate. Stimming might be: dancing, clapping, tapping, clicking fingers, vocalising, stretching, singing, rocking; there can even be visual stims too.

References

- acerbecky (2015) 'Interview with Dr Wenn Lawson, to mark World Autism Awareness Day, 2015,' https://acertheblog.wordpress.com/2015/04/01/interview-with-dr-wenn-lawson-to-mark-world-autism-awareness-day-2015.
- Cambridge Dictionary (n.d. a) 'Autonomy,' https://dictionary.cambridge.org/dictionary/english/autonomy.
- Cambridge Dictionary (n.d. b) 'Circadian clock,' https://dictionary.cambridge.org/dictionary/english/circadian-clock.
- Cambridge Dictionary (n.d. c) 'Stigmatization,' https://dictionary.cambridge.org/dictionary/english/stigmatization.
- Crompton, C.J. et al. (2021) 'Double empathy: why autistic people are often misunderstood,' *Frontiers for Young Minds*, 9.
- Faculty of Philosophy, University of Oxford (n.d.) 'Empathy,' www.philosophy.ox.ac.uk/what-empathy.
- Milton, D. (2018) 'The double empathy problem,' National Autistic Society, www.autism.org.uk/advice-and-guidance/professional-practice/double-empathy.
- Raymaker, D.M. et al. (2020) '"Having all of your internal resources exhausted beyond measure and being left with no clean-up crew": defining autistic burnout,' *Autism in Adulthood*, 2(2), 132–143.
- Stimpunks Foundation (n.d.) 'Home page,' https://stimpunks.org/glossary/neurodivergent.
- Walker, N. (n.d.) 'Neurodiversity: Some Basic Terms & Definitions,' https://neuroqueer.com/neurodiversity-terms-and-definitions.